Inside Story

Inside Story

How Narratives Drive Mass Harm

Lois Presser

UNIVERSITY OF CALIFORNIA PRESS

University of California Press, one of the most distinguished university presses in the United States, enriches lives around the world by advancing scholarship in the humanities, social sciences, and natural sciences. Its activities are supported by the UC Press Foundation and by philanthropic contributions from individuals and institutions. For more information, visit www.ucpress.edu.

University of California Press
Oakland, California

Library of Congress Cataloging-in-Publication Data

Names: Presser, Lois, author.
Title: Inside story : how narratives drive mass harm / Lois Presser.
Description: Oakland, California : University of California Press, [2018] | Includes bibliographical references and index. |
Identifiers: lccn 2018017428 (print) | lccn 2018020178 (ebook) | isbn 9780520964471 (ebook) | isbn 9780520290174 (cloth : alk. paper) | isbn 9780520290181 (pbk. : alk. paper)
Subjects: lcsh: Crime—Sociological aspects. | Crime in popular culture. | Criminal psychology. | Violence.
Classification: lcc hv6025 (ebook) | lcc hv6025 .p664 2018 (print) | ddc 303.6—dc23
LC record available at https://lccn.loc.gov/2018017428

27 26 25 24 23 22 21 20 19 18
10 9 8 7 6 5 4 3 2 1

CONTENTS

PREFACE

The populism that has enraptured large segments of the populations of democratic societies is a main source of inspiration for this book. The question that is central to the book—What accounts for the emotional grip of stories?—is a question I want to ask of the current popular movements that support autocracy, nativism, and racism. If ever a historical moment presented itself as requiring a sociological exploration of ideologically powered zeal, that moment is now.

Donald J. Trump was elected president of the United States when I was nearing completion of the book. Both during the presidential campaign in 2016 and after the election, in 2017, stories swirled—about Trump and his rival Hillary Clinton, foreign interference in electoral politics, corruption, treason, election fraud, tax fraud, corporate greed, secret surveillance, child sexual abuse, adult sexual abuse, government regulations and jobs, terrorists and other criminals crossing our borders, and about who and what America is and ought to be and what Americans need. No narrative was too far-fetched or improbable. We are spellbound by the stories of our times, both the stories we judge to be false and those we judge to be true. And we are stunned by the discovery—a new one, it seems, for a broad public and even many political experts—of the real-world impacts of people's stories.

If the spectacle and impact of today's stories have stimulated my thinking, they have also at times been exhausting. For deeply felt support I want to thank Linda and Larry Blair, Michelle Brown, Michelle Christian, Julia Chu, Reuben Danzing, Emily Gaarder, Carol Nickle, Joey Presser, and Jon Shefner. My resistance friends Jenny Jones, Deloris Mabins, and Charlene Negendank and my Heska Amuna community have truly sustained me.

I am also indebted to the International Society for the Study of Narrative for literature recommendations, to the Culture and Animals Foundation for financial support, and to the University of Tennessee for a faculty development leave. I gained immeasurably from a month in residence at the University of Oslo alongside Sveinung Sandberg, Thomas Ugelvik, and Ingvild Knævelsrud Rabe, and many wonderful others, of that fine institution. Maura Roessner of the University of California Press was unsparing with encouragement and guidance.

I am especially grateful to my children, Ansel and Halen Presser, and glad for the story we are developing together about fairness, compassion, and love.

CHAPTER ONE

Introduction

Narratives and Narrative Impacts

In October 2016 a story began circulating online about goings-on at Comet Ping Pong, a Washington, DC, pizza restaurant. According to the story, the restaurant was a staging ground for a human trafficking and child sex abuse operation run by presidential candidate Hillary Clinton and her campaign manager. On December 4, 2016, a North Carolina man named Edgar Welch stormed the restaurant with an assault rifle and took aim at employees, intent on rescuing the abused children and exposing the operation (Kang and Goldman 2016).

The tales people hear and tell inspire them to take action that is more or less consequential and more or less bold. We vote, demonstrate, and perpetrate violence on the basis of shifting accounts of being in the world. We also choose jobs, friends, and life partners; decide where to live and which groups to join; and decide to quit, alter, endure, or appreciate whatever path we have chosen. Remarkably, stories get masses of people to believe in and commit to the same things. What gives stories their power? This book explores the capacity of stories, or narratives, to nurture the motivation both to perpetrate harm and to ignore harm done by others.[1] The book builds *narrative criminology*, or the study of the relationship between narratives and harmful actions and patterns (Presser 2009; Presser and Sandberg 2015). My goal is to suggest precise ways of thinking about how narratives promote actions and specifically though not exclusively harmful actions in which large numbers are affected and large numbers are implicated.

As far as arousal goes, there is nothing special about the story that motivates our participation in harm-doing, as opposed to other stories. I am roused, for instance, by a story of having neglected a friend, compelling me to send her a gift. This book sets aside the nature or content of harmgenic stories in order to concentrate on mechanisms of narrative sway.

NARRATIVE IMMERSION

Those who study reading, mostly literary scholars and psychologists, observe that we get "lost" in (Nell 1988) or "seduced" (Chambers 1984) or "transported" (Gerrig 1993) by narratives. Reading can put us into a sort of "trance," hence the "witchery" of stories (Gottschall 2012; Nell 1988). When we are absorbed in this way, we notice fewer inaccuracies in the story, and we evaluate protagonists more positively (Green and Brock 2000). Green, Garst, and Brock (2004) propose that narrative operates "as a cue to a reader to engage in a less-critical, more immersive form of mental engagement" (p. 165). The experience of "immersion in narratives brings about partial isolation from the facts of the real world" (Gerrig 1993, p. 16). Beyond ideational impacts, those who research narrative impacts emphasize emotional arousal (Harold 2005; Hogan 2003; A.M. Jacobs 2015; Nabi and

Green 2015; Oatley 2002; Polichak and Gerrig 2002; Tan 1996). Indeed, narrative's emotional influence may be preeminent, as Green and Brock (2002) state: "Individuals are swept away by a story, and thus come to believe in ideas suggested by the narrative" (p. 325). A good story gets us feeling excited, anxious, disgusted, saddened, or satisfied. We identify and empathize with fictional characters: we come to feel what they feel (J. Cohen 2001; cf. Keen 2007). Absorbed in fiction, we become active participants in the storied events (Iser 1972, 1978; Polichak and Gerrig 2002).

Scholarly investigation of narrative impacts deals mainly with the verbal arts, or literature. It concerns fictional stories recounted by others almost exclusively. But comparable impacts are evident whether the story is fiction or nonfiction (Green, Garst, and Brock 2004; Strange and Leung 1999) and whether the story is received or told. Hence Torossian's (1937) assertion: "The difference ... between aesthetic and practical emotional experience is not very great. The same psychological factors of memory and association, as well as those already discussed, are involved in both; except that in a practical experience the feelings aroused are identified with the individual having the experience, whereas in an aesthetic experience the feelings aroused are identified with the contemplated object" (p. 25). A storied reality takes hold of us at all times. And we regularly tell stories about ourselves, in the form of statements we make self-consciously and the internal and "virtually uninterrupted monologue" of which we are barely conscious (Brooks 1984, p. 3). Psychologist Victor Nell (1988) notes that "a narrative continues to exercise its fascination if teller and audience are condensed into one person and the act of telling is reduced to silence" (p. 61).

It is in fact likely that we are even more susceptible to the impact of self-stories (or we-stories) than we are to *other* people's stories. Engagement in the latter requires, at a minimum, an interest in whoever the story is about and what they are going through (Schank and Berman 2002). Yet, we are predictably interested in ourselves and in the real-world narratives in which we cast ourselves. We care about the outcomes of such narratives, and we identify with the protagonist as a matter of course.

CAPTIVATING THE SELF

For some, the idea that we could captivate ourselves might seem bizarre. Not so for the medical researchers whose randomized trials bear out the effectiveness of self-hypnosis on pain and health-related attitudes, among other things. We very effectively cast spells on ourselves *by* ourselves with no one else to distract us. As for stories, neuroscientists observe that most of the same regions of the brain and mental processes are involved when we construct and when we absorb narratives (see, e.g., Mar 2004; Silbert et al. 2014). Both processes demand the ability to order propositions to construct meaning, and both rely on the ability to divine other people's (characters') mental states—that is, to conjure theory of mind.

In addition, both in telling and in processing stories we rely on shared prototypes (Hogan 2003), which brings us to another basis for susceptibility to our own stories. "Our" stories are never completely our own. They draw on "recognizable plots, character types, conventional tropes, genre-specific cues that build suspense" (Frank 2010a, p. 119). Thus, when we inspire ourselves, the ultimate source of the inspiration is collective. The cultural resources we use for telling stories are the same ones we use for understanding stories. Imagine, for example, my story of a recent breakup along lines of failing to see clearly how frayed the bonds I shared with my partner truly were the whole time we were together. The unseeing protagonist is a conventional character in our culture, the unwelcome revelation a conventional plotline. This story is no less compelling to me and to others for its conventionality.

If notions of trance and witchery seem foreign to *criminology*, consider our homegrown theories of the morally bankrupt crowd, the drift into juvenile delinquency, and the spectacle of crime. Gustav Le Bon (1903) observed that individuals relinquish thinking to the crowd; the individual "is no longer himself, but has become an automaton who has ceased to be guided by his will" (p. 24), hence "the hypnotizing effect of general beliefs" (p. 141). The crowd is unreasonable; it buys into "the most improbable legends and stories" (p. 32). In David Matza's (1964) theory of drift, the young person gets carried away and into offending. Drift is "a gradual process of movement, unperceived by the actor" (p. 29), an "episodic release from moral constraint" (p. 69). Today's cultural criminologists account for punishment, crime, and other transgressions in terms of energy and verve, underwritten by shared semiotics. For example, Mike Presdee (2000) took note of trances achieved by youth in club culture, who through music and drugs make "pleasure the site of meaning" (p. 122). These scholars and others (e.g., Gadd and Jefferson 2007; McLaughlin 2014) grapple with the suspension of human reasoning in the context of transgression and violence.

Under the spell of narrative one's reasoning is not so much suspended as it is altered. Narrative itself is said to be a *way* of reasoning—temporally, causally, and meaningfully (Bruner 1986). Research from experimental psychology shows that we are active thinkers even when—or *as*—we are absorbed in narrative (see Gerrig 1993; Nell 1988). Furthermore, we get absorbed within certain social settings and times and phases of life, and not others. A theory based on narrative can expound the nature of getting swept away and into doing harm while not abandoning the idea that individuals are agents living in social contexts who make choices. To properly build such a theory we need, in addition to an account of narrative, an account of emotion. Martha Nussbaum (2001) and Paul Colm Hogan (2003) offer especially useful theories for present purposes.

Nussbaum (2001) identifies emotions as appraisals that "ascribe to things and persons outside the person's own control great importance for that person's own flourishing" (p. 4). Feelings reflect an interpretation of events and circumstances that highlights issues of control and well-being. Even as Nussbaum traces emotional experience to "propositional content" concerning a particular present experience and especially a loss or a triumph, she notes that such experience "involves a storm of memories and concrete perceptions that swarm around that content, but add more than is present in it" (p. 65). Raw material for the felt experience of our appraisals is past experience rendered imaginatively. Hogan (2003) takes the view that our most basic concepts of emotion are rooted in universal stories that relay both eliciting conditions and the effects of feeling some feeling. Thus are narrative and emotion "almost inseparable phenomena" (p. 264). Enriched by insights from cognitive science and Sanskrit literary theory, Hogan argues that stories' suggestive shading of meaning activates traces of memories and thereupon the emotions associated with these. Both scholars tie feeling to signification through the lens of the past. Hogan furthermore conceptualizes shared narratives as engines of signification and credits narrative ambiguity with provocation. Nussbaum is more attentive to the beguiling theme of control over well-being.

What remains necessary for theorizing *mass* arousal is some sociology of cognition, for as Hagan and Rymond-Richmond (2009) remind us, "a collective explanation is needed for collective violence" (p. 136). Stories act upon multitudes. The cognitive and emotional impacts I am concerned with are communal ones. The work of Eviatar Zerubavel (1997) fills in here, highlighting the enculturation of major processes of cognition, including classification and memory. Of particular relevance to collective narratives: Zerubavel demonstrates that our memories are as likely to be located in impersonal sites as they are in embodied, personal ones. We can begin to grasp how narratives impact aggregates by recognizing that many of the deep associations through which we know the world are shared. I will contemplate the collective rememberings and forgettings through which stories resonate.

Story-making and storytelling are processes, of course. Styles of storytelling shape the "involvement" of interlocutors and audiences (Tannen 1989). Compelling cadence, use of repetition, alliteration and parataxis, posing rhetorical questions, and the like make speech, not merely stories, affecting and persuasive. Of particular sociological relevance: contexts for telling stories, as Polletta (2006) demonstrates, "determine what kind of a hearing particular stories secure" (p. 167). We are more apt to listen to individuals with power, those who stand on the so-called bully pulpit. Whether one's story is accepted, and thus whether it has social influence, also depends on whether one has abided by setting-specific norms of storytelling: for example, in criminal courts "true stories remain identical in their retelling" (Polletta 2006, p. 167), a convention relaxed elsewhere. In addition, in real-time communication interlocutors shape the narrative that "one" tells and the impact that the narrative has on the interlocutors in turn (Presser 2009). Whether a story "speaks" to us and whether we make a popular story "our own" depends on all of these factors.

Reading theorists' take on active participant involvement pertains here. Broadly, they stress that we bring our own storied experiences and positions, both attitudinal and structural, to the cultural encounter that is reading (e.g., Iser 1978). McDonnell, Bail, and Tavory's (2017) theory of resonance also points to interpretation as actively undertaken. They state: "It is thus only through the effect of signs that meaning-making is completed, and such effect cannot be encapsulated by an analysis of cultural objects but must also take into account the habits of thought and action through which an interpreter experiences such an object" (p. 3).

Recognizing that narrative, like other cultural forms, is a product of social processes, my analysis of narrative influence nonetheless brackets process. I want to say something about the stuff and the structure of narrative that animate action as well as inaction. I want to address why narrative, among cultural forms, is exceptional at propulsion and to determine "the sensible properties" of some narrative that make it especially propulsive (Matravers 1991, p. 329). However, I can only sideline narrative exchange for so long. I consider both what is said and what is not said as exerting an aesthetic impact, and the "not said" especially obviously requires an interpreting agent for impact. The stories we tell ourselves draw on both novel/situated and prefabricated understandings.

Preparing to make sense of narrative arousal, this introductory chapter summarizes the narrative criminological view of stories as grounds for action, explores the question of narrative truth within the context of narrative impact, and outlines the book.

THE STORIED GROUNDS OF ACTION

Narrative criminologists are mostly concerned with the nefarious effects of stories, or how they condition patterns of criminal and criminalized action.[2] Narrative criminology is broadly framed by the symbolic interactionist and social constructionist perspectives within sociology, that we act based on meanings assigned to things. We respond to some version of the world and not to the world per se. Berger and Luckmann (1966, p. 37), key architects of that perspective, observe that social construction work is discursive by nature: "The common objectivations of everyday life are maintained primarily by linguistic signification. Everyday life is, above all, life with and by means of the language I share with my fellowmen. An understanding of language is thus essential for any understanding of the reality of everyday life." Heeding the call for linguistic proficiency, social researchers have highlighted the reality-producing effects of pragmatics such as implied or presupposed meanings, mechanics of communication such as grammar, and structures, including figurative devices and narrative. Discourse analysis is one name for the family of approaches these efforts take.[3] The basic premise of discourse analysis is that discourse matters to *action*. Whereas that assumption is often unstated and unexamined, in various corners of the social sciences it has undergone empirical demonstration.

Within criminology, narrative criminologists have pioneered this work. They take two approaches to the narrative-action relationship. They either view narratives as suggesting how people should act or guiding action, *or* they view action as a performance of a particular self-narrative. Or they adopt both views, for though distinguishable, these approaches are not mutually exclusive within a particular research project. Both the guiding and the identity-performative perspectives on narrative give an indication of how meanings packaged as stories influence our behavior in ways that other discursive forms do not.

Framing and Guiding

Narratives help us interpret circumstances and events, and those interpretations guide how we respond. One of the principal functions of narratives is to make moral meaning of situations and events. Therefore, it is not surprising that so much research fleshing out the idea of narratives as guides has been done in the areas of social (e.g., protest) movements and criminology. Research on the role of narratives in social movements follows important work on frames, which "function to organize experience and guide action" (Snow et al. 1986, p. 464). This body of work advances a view of frames as shared mental schemes, of what people "are alive to" (Goffman 1974, p. 8) in a situation. Framing scholars always did make reference to discourse and are increasingly devoting even more attention to narrative discourse in particular. Collective constructions of grievances, their causes, responsible parties, and victims evidently take the form of narratives (J.E. Davis 2002; Fine 2002; R.N. Jacobs 2002; Loseke 2003; Polletta 2006). For example, movement organizers present claims in narrative form in order to mobilize participation. Narratives play a decisive role in representing actions whose rightness is questionable (Scott and

Lyman 1968). Philip Smith's (2005) insistence on the fundamentally storied signification of designs to wage war showcases that role:

> The image of an objectively identifiable "enemy" who is subsequently "demonized" by a post facto cultural process or "interests" that need "explanation" to the public is fundamentally mistaken. The "enemy" and "interests" require cultural patterns for their very recognition. In a sense they are talked into relevance—but not existence—through the storytelling, genre guessing dialogical activities of the public sphere. Likewise, any "threats" that need to be dealt with require identification, prioritizing, and evaluation. Here too we have seen that cultural resources are needed: frameworks that allow clues to be assembled and efforts made to guess likely costs and benefits to military action or inaction. (p. 209)

Smith's approach may be contrasted with one centered on propaganda or spin, with which dubious policies are sold to the masses. The concept of propaganda does not go far enough to depict the *fundamental* shaping role of discourse in preparing a group to inflict harm by constructing values, goals, and "truths" about experience and parties to it. In addition, narratives characterize actors, patients, and action, whereas propaganda is more generic as to focus.

War and other mass harms that we call violent are typically promoted by stories of a virtuous protagonist facing off against a malevolent other whose forceful overcoming is necessary for salvation. For example, war enemies are "encoded as polluted," whereas "we" are "encoded as pure" (P. Smith 2005, p. 27). But this is just one manifestation of the general harm logic of *reduction* of targets, according to which they are cast as having few interests or we project our own interests onto them (Presser 2013). How we construct targets is imperative because the most murderous among us is not generically aggressive but rather aggressive toward particular beings, under some conditions and not others. In the case of mass "violence" we reduce the target to an enemy bent on persecuting or otherwise hurting us. In cases of mass negligence or legal, institutionalized destruction, the target is a simplified and marginalized group or species. We also construct ourselves in terms of capacities, rights, duties, and so forth.

Performativity

The symbolic interactionist perspective has generated a second way of theorizing the discursive grounds of action, one that has action writing or constituting the subject. Instead of acting within a world whose meaning has been forged by stories, one acts to make a story come true. The interest is in meaning-making as opposed to meaning "effects." One good example of "acting for the story" comes from Curtis Jackson-Jacobs's (2004) study of young men who start street fights, including ones they are unlikely to win. They thrill to the prospect of such violence. Jackson-Jacobs explains: "Fighters intend their brawls to make good stories that reveal themselves as charismatic. And so they enact storylines that they expect will both test their character and be applauded by audiences" (p. 232). Jackson-Jacobs refers to narrative "gratifications" and "payoffs," especially the thrill of realizing "a storied self: a self that will become publicly and enduringly admired, immortalised in epic fight stories told for years to come" (p. 231). Jack Katz (1988) makes a similar point about enacting a rewarding story even when the action might be lethal. Katz observes, for example, that for murderers "the dramaturgic aspects of the fatal scenes were specifically appealing"

(p. 300). He explains: "The key emotional dynamic on the path to these ('senseless') murders is a play with moral symbolics in which (1) the protagonist enters as a pariah, (2) soon becomes lost in the dizzying symbolics of deviance, and then (3) emerges to reverse the equation in a violent act of transcendence" (p. 290). As in Jackson-Jacobs's research, violent action permits Katz's actor to perform a preferred self-story and thereby to construct a sought-after identity—a desired character. Another broadly significant case of acting for the story has institutional agents (e.g., states, militias, and law enforcement) manipulating their practices in order to construct themselves as triumphant, fierce, and so forth. The conceptual shift here is to conceive of the institution as a character with a public image. Thus we find police officials instructing officers to make more arrests in order to present the agency as tough on (and effective against) crime, and state regimes implementing policy as political theater.

In both the micro- and macro-level identity-performative cases the agent's cognition is sidelined. Narrative is less how we know the world than it is a vehicle for being known in the world. The acting-for-the-story perspective posits stories as resources for identity-constructing persons rather than as guides to action; hence it takes the desire to realize a particular story or identity to be foundational. We act for the sake of a story; we do not act *based on* stories.

The identity-performative perspective on narrative has obvious affinities with Goffman's (1959) dramaturgical theory of social action and the doing gender approach (Butler 1990; Messerschmidt 1997; C. West and Zimmerman 1987). It is compatible with cultural criminology, for which crime and other transgressions as well as "criminal justice" are creative processes of meaning-making (Ferrell et al. 2004). The emphasis throughout is on action or practice, which communicates but is not textual in the technical sense of that word. The contributions of this view include its foregrounding of identity, gender identity not least of all; its recognition that we are always sending messages about ourselves to ourselves and to other people; and its provocative formulation of social action as signifying in the first instance. Yet, my inquiry into narrative immersion and impact does not easily align itself with the identity-performative perspective. A culturally favored narrative is already solidly in place from this theoretical position; therefore, the precise workings of that narrative (and how they may change) are not specified. The particulars of narratives have no special relevance to the theory; it may not be possible even to discuss narrative impacts. Going forward, I am keen to unpack the seductions of narrative that inspire crime and other harm, rather than the "seductions of crime" (Katz 1988) as story-making. Here I want to reiterate that these approaches are not logically incompatible. Actions may be "planned to generate an already imagined story of those actions" (Frank 2010a, p. 132), *and* the story may shape how people, including those who conceived it, think and feel. Storytelling may be seen as both strategic and impactful, something we manipulate and something that manipulates us.

NARRATIVE TRUTH AND NARRATIVE IMPACT

The supposed falsehood of certain stories has, in my view, been a distraction to narrative inquiry within criminology (Presser 2016). It has been presumed that only "real" things cause crime. Hence, many analysts who collect and/or appreciate narrative data seek to verify the authenticity of what the narrator has reported. But narratives affect us whether or not they are "true."[4]

Gerrig (1993) writes: "With respect to the cognitive activities of readers, the experience of narratives is largely unaffected by their announced correspondence with reality" (p. 102). Inaccuracies and even outright duplicity therefore should not prevent social researchers from taking stories seriously.

What do we mean by truth? A story is generally called true if it corresponds to some verified reality. False stories are said to be discordant with that reality: they advance untruths or omit essential facts. A general suspicion regarding the truthfulness of harmdoers' stories prevails in part because stories are used to explain one's actions—which include actions held to be unethical. Those held liable for their actions tell stories: the motivation exists to be dishonest in order to get out of trouble and/or to continue doing what they are doing. But stories, always retrospective, also point forward. They give shape to what one will do next. The productivity of stories, rather than their epistemological basis, is what narrativists in the social sciences are wont to expose.

That factual accuracy does not determine the power of narratives should be quite evident from recent world affairs. Consider Pizzagate, the "fake" but influential online news story of Hillary Clinton's pedophile enterprise mentioned at the launch of this chapter. Consider too the more or less fanciful tales used to recruit child soldiers, incite genocides, gain spiritual followers, or outpace political competitors. Stories that cast doubt on anthropogenic climate change take liberties even with established facts, but the impact of those stories cannot be denied. Nor does the accuracy of my personal or mundane stories matter, such as the one I tell myself of someone cutting me off on the road or leaving the milk out overnight. However untrue, they make me angry in the event. The turbulent 2016 race for president of the United States made abundantly clear that supporters open themselves to the influence of even outlandish stories that they want to believe (see, e.g., Gabriel 2016; Kang and Goldman 2016). Rapid-fire proliferation of information through technological innovation may have primed people to prioritize believability over accuracy on the idea that truth is difficult to nail down. Yet, it has been noted for some time that, among other things, a story's verisimilitude or believability rather than its actual truthfulness determines its impact (Bruner 1986; Busselle and Bilandzic 2008). Emotion scholars agree that it is "the impression of reality created in the subject" and not objective reality that evokes feeling (Tan 1996, p. 67).

I have been discussing examples of stories that recipients *believe* to be *true*. We are led to wonder, though: Are we affected by stories that we *believe* to be *false*? The question has special relevance in the face of seemingly cynical political leadership. Do leaders—does anyone—believe their own duplicitous accounts?

Research demonstrates that we are affected by stories we know to be *fictional* (Green and Brock 2000; Green, Garst, and Brock 2004; Oatley 1999; Strange and Leung 1999). Impacts of the novel *Uncle Tom's Cabin* on nineteenth-century American society (Hanne 1994) and of Richard Wagner's operas on Adolf Hitler (Gottschall 2012) are well documented.[5] Experimental research demonstrates stories' effect on readers' attitudes whether or not the stories are designated as fact or fiction. Few would call fiction false, but neither is it true in the technical sense of reporting on the real-world experiences of real-world individuals.[6] In fiction, "*something* is consciously and openly 'feigned'" (Strange 2002, p. 265; emphasis in original).

Are we also affected by the false story that calls itself nonfiction—what Kermode (1967, p. 190) calls a myth as opposed to a fiction? The notion of true (or false) nonfiction stories is, in fact, far from straightforward. Accounts of experience in the real world are molded by the unreliable reconstruction of memory, the requirement of adapting to cultural templates and demands, a desire to make ourselves (story protagonists) look good, the requirement of tailoring the story to imagined audiences and the active influence of interlocutors at hand. All stories are selective in which facts they include; they cannot possibly include everything. Faithful copy may be pursued but it is never actually achieved. These considerations connect to the post-structuralist critique of the notion of stories "out there" awaiting representation. In short, truth as commonly construed is an impracticable standard for storytellers.

I suspect, though, that when we question the truth of a nonfictional story, we have in mind a self-interested storyteller who is keeping something under wraps for which the story is cover. We suspect an ulterior motive for telling the story. In fact, most communication is geared toward purposes other than simply to deliver information (Austin 1962). I might tell you a woeful story from my childhood to enlighten you as to my background while also (or actually) trying to bond with you or to make you feel guilty for some slight. I feel no qualms about not revealing this other motive, and my society makes no demands that I do; indeed, it would seem strange if I did. We should thus set aside the idea that having purposes for storytelling beyond sharing makes the story suspect.

Suppose, though, that a story *is* told in bad faith. Are cynical storytellers affected by their false stories—those that package disinformation? That my insincere story influences me derives first from the fact that I am held to act accountably to it. Social sanctions befall those whose narrative is discrepant with what they do. In the short or long run, political leaders are held accountable for the narratives they tell by those who believed them and by those who did not: consider U.S. president George W. Bush being taken to task for lying about Iraq's president Saddam Hussein having weapons of mass destruction (Stein and Dickinson 2006).[7] Stories, like all other communicative devices, make commitments: the stories we tell obligate us to varying degrees. If our stories lack conformity with intersubjectively supposed truth, other people's trust in us breaks down.

In addition and more to the concern of this book, we ourselves are impacted by what we say and do. Drawing that lesson from various experiments, Daryl Bem (1972) formulated self-perception theory: we infer what we are like and what we believe from our actions. For example, in forbidden toy studies, children who were merely told to avoid playing with a toy or face mild punishment subsequently rejected the toy more than did those who had been threatened with more severe punishment for playing with it. Bem reasons: "If [the participant] has refrained from playing with the toy under severe threat, he can still infer that he may like the toy, but if he has refrained under mild threat, then he could conclude that he must not like the toy" (pp. 20–21). In other words, people gather information about themselves from situational cues, and "private stimuli probably play a smaller role in self-description than we have come to believe" (p. 4). When people say something under conditions lacking obvious coercion, punishment, or reward, they may infer that they are being truthful even to themselves. So, when Jim David Adkisson, alone in his duplex apartment prior to a mass shooting spree at a Tennessee church, wrote his manifesto explaining that he was upset by Democrats, he is likely to have believed he was, whatever his original state (Presser 2012). At the least, that discursive action fortified his belief. Similarly, although those who tell stories asserting racial superiority or denying climate change may be foundationally motivated to do so for material and/or so-called political reasons, they might come to believe their disingenuous stories anyway.[8]

To summarize, stories, including ones told dishonestly, affect us. But we should not rest with the observation that narratives get to us: we should ask *how* they do it.

INVESTIGATING NARRATIVE IMPACTS

The present study addresses a question the gist of which has been posed by scholars across the academy. Cognitive psychologist Richard Gerrig (1993) takes note of "how little is known about the 'dimensions' of narrative experience—that is the theory of aesthetics that remains undeveloped" (p. 175). Social psychologists Melanie Green and Timothy Brock (2002) remark on how "little attention has been paid to the specific processes by which narrative or fictional communications might have persuasive effects" (p. 316). Literary scholar Jonathan Gottschall (2012) observes: "There is still a lot to be discovered about the extent and magnitude of story's sculpting power" (p. 152). We know that narratives drive collective action and need more information. Why does a story of injustice, degradation, triumph against the odds, or anything else provoke us?

I will tease out both the features that make stories generally impactful and those that make some stories more impactful than others. By impactful, let me be clear, I mean nurturing an emotional response, which may be something on the order of tranquillity, and not merely passion, rage, exhilaration, and the like. My main argument is that the most commanding stories remind us of the precariousness of our existence and offer hope of unremitting control and infinite existence or at least infinite significance. Their resolution is a recognizably stable self.

The five chapters that follow amount to an investigation of how narrative may drive mass harm. I take mass harm to be any practice in which many people are implicated which causes the suffering of many. Examples of mass harm include terrorism, counterterrorism, animal abuse, imprisonment, systematic sexual violence and tolerance thereof, slavery, war-making, and genocide. These harms are not equivalent, and I am not concerned to classify them except insofar as stories do. My aim is to clarify the ways stories influence thoughts and feelings which in turn encourage a variety of harms.

Chapter 2 examines the discursive processes that support mass harm and amasses a body of evidence of narrative impacts on mass harm. Case studies of mass harm reveal figurative expressions and narratives to be highly consequential. These studies tend to emphasize framing and thus legitimization of action. Figurative language, especially metaphors, and narratives set out harm agents as heroic or decent, harm-doing as acceptable or virtuous, and targets of harm as deserving or beyond concern. The overarching message of this body of work is that language powers action via its capacity to shape propositional content and its uptake. My review opens up the question for the rest of the book of what gives narratives engendering harm their emotional and thus motivating force.

Chapter 3 investigates the affective charge of narrative. It asks why narrative in general invites immersion and why some narratives are especially inviting. The answer I arrive at implicates narrative capacities for integrating meanings, constructing and—especially through story endings—putting a stop to dynamic agency, and moralizing experience. I draw heavily on cognitive theories of emotion, which tie emotion to one's evaluation of experiences as important to one's well-being. Nussbaum (2001) emphasizes the emotional aspect of issues of control over well-being. Nussbaum as well as Hogan (2003) help to clarify the density of emotion in terms of past experience, but I also discern an aesthetic pull from narrative as figurative device and (thus) site of ambiguity. Something about obscure messaging pulls us in. Becker's (1973) theory of death denial allows consideration of narrative meaning for all time as a salve to existential anxiety. I conclude this chapter by developing the position that narrative arousal is a function of narrative's capacity for holistic synthesis of experience and identity, which, paradoxically, depends in part on the indeterminacy of meaning (hence meaning of the self). Different stories provoke emotional reactions of varying force and engagement, from a sense of urgency to a mood of satisfaction, depending on how much preferred experiences and identities are under threat.

Chapters 4 and 5 apply these ideas to two rather different social spheres and narratives. They represent extremes of emotional engagement—dramatic versus dispassionate—in stories that underpin mass harm.

Chapter 4 makes sense of the draw of underdog stories in which humble and seemingly ineffectual but righteous heroes triumph in this world or in the eternal one, over mighty adversaries. The chapter draws on several empirical examples—religious parables, the film *Rocky*, antiabortion activism, and anti-LGBT activism. The underdog story rouses its audiences on the basis of assurances that heroes come under divine protection, that they are connected to but unique among fellows, and that their deeds have transcendent importance. The story declares its end with the hero's triumph, thus denying adversaries future agency.

In chapter 5 certain narratives are shown to foster a mood of satisfaction, which presents as indifference to harms perpetrated by others. We are moved to accept the status quo or some set of arrangements carried out in our names. Here I analyze an influential criminological narrative, the so-called general theory of crime by Gottfredson and Hirschi (1990), which relates how individuals become criminals through negligent parenting. The narrative allows us to construct everlastingly good selves in contrast to irresponsible and inconsequential others and charts a path to our control, over self and others, in this lifetime. Whether dramatic or subdued, stories that fuel mass harm draw contrasts that reassure audiences of their morally right positions. I am in that audience, a fact that chapter 5 highlights. I am a sociological criminologist who is accustomed to pondering rather dispassionately the harms heaped upon criminalized persons, their families, and their communities. I am concerned about these harms, but I am also regularly able to set aside my concern. My affect when I think about penal harm is usually subdued, and my record of activism is, sadly, spotty. By theorizing the emotional impacts of the story of antisociality, I am in effect investigating my own comfort level.

Chapter 6 summarizes the aesthetic nature of destructive narrative influence, draws out theoretical implications, and identifies points of potential intervention based on the analysis—resisting certain stories and telling new ones that encourage "life-enhancing illusions" (Becker 1973, p. 158) rather than illusions that degrade and destroy.

CHAPTER TWO

The Cultural Grounds of Mass Harm

Large-scale projects that cause suffering, degrade, and destroy—war, massacre, state torture, slavery, lynching, pogroms, human trafficking, terrorism, counterterrorism, prostitution, criminal punishment, economic exploitation, political repression, environmental degradation, industrialized agriculture, meat eating, and so on—are commonly explained in terms of quests to win or maximize resources and power. These projects and the struggles and objectives they pursue are also always coded symbolically. That is to say, mass harm is enculturated. It is naturalized, normalized, trivialized, excused, justified, commended, and/or obfuscated. These and other processes of enculturation are discursive.[1] They are bound to language, to the way people talk about them. To build a case for the discursive grounds of mass harm in this chapter, I first reflect on the nature of mass harm and address why mass harm in particular warrants a cultural analysis. Then I examine scholarship linking mass harm to cognition and processes that manipulate (1) cognitive processes, as well as discursive forms, which I distinguish as (2) wording or (3) narratives. This review leads me to suggest that narratives are uniquely effective vehicles for moral and thus emotional messaging. Yet, research on mass harm, highlighting narrative or anything else, has clarified processes of legitimation to the virtual neglect of emotional inspiration.

CONCEPTUALIZING MASS HARM

The special concern of this book is mass harm. It is crucial that we comprehend how devastation *actually* mounts up—against criminology's traditional preoccupation with individual action in violation of some law. I define *harm* as trouble caused by another. Intent to harm is not essential to this definition, though actors "must have had some notion that their (in)action might result in harm" (Presser 2013, p. 7).

My definition depends on some agent naming some experience as "trouble." Questions of who that agent should be and which alleged troubles necessitate concern are admittedly problematic, as demonstrated by competing claims of victimhood in the context of sexual misconduct (i.e., pointing to damaged souls and careers). Yet, as scores of critical criminologists have maintained, "crime" is no less problematic a concept. A focus on crime privileges the perspective of lawmakers and law enforcement agents, while "harm" takes seriously the felt consequences of action.[2]

What is *mass* harm, then? Its parameters are not transparent. Mass incarceration means large numbers of people incarcerated, mass murder means large numbers murdered, and so on. Logically, then, mass harm should mean masses *harmed*, and it does. I propose, furthermore, that mass harm entails mass *involvement*. If many are victimized, many are implicated. Mass harm requires multiple agents who may bear widely differing levels of responsibility, but nonetheless bear responsibility. Conceivably, one person could fly a drone that launches a missile or dump the toxins that annihilate an ocean's marine life. However, the motivated agent needs others to manufacture and supply the tools to harm and to escape detection. Harms under fascism seem to emanate from a single leader, but the fascist ruler needs henchmen. Besides, today's mass surveillance, instant communication, and global capital both check and facilitate our actions. Then there is the motivation to harm in the first place. If recent "lone wolf" terrorist attacks tell us anything, it is that the inspiration to do mass harm is usually communally sourced (Berntzen and Sandberg 2014). Of genocide Savelsberg (2010) observes: "Grave human rights violations can only be understood as the outcome of collective or organizational, especially state, action" (p. 51). Individual aggressors are heavily in debt to their social milieu (see also Bandura 1999).

To conceptualize mass harm as mass *involvement* in harm is to make a controversial move. Elites and the rest of us, it seems, would like to deflect and concentrate responsibility. A case in point is present-day denials of institutional complicity in sexual harassment and rape. Stewards of churches, schools, businesses, fraternities, the military, and other spaces from which survivors have come forward regularly reject the notion that their cultures are enabling, despite disproportionately high rates of victimization in those spaces. Such denials are no doubt meant to preserve power. But I believe they also stem from a failure to grasp the expansiveness of the enculturation of social life.

The commonplace harms just mentioned as well as the atrocities of the twentieth century make it painfully clear that mass harm requires "standing by" as much as it does actively inflicting the harm. Hence the lucidity of the statement attributed to Edmund Burke: "The only thing necessary for the triumph of evil is for good men to do nothing." Perpetration receives the lion's share of attention, however, both in popular culture and, less defensibly, in the field of criminology (Manji, Presser, and Dickey 2014). A cultural approach to mass harm is able to account for both perpetration (from administration to manual involvement) and failure of intervention: cultural processes—ideas, figurative expressions (e.g., metaphors), and stories—are aimed at and influence both direct agents and bystanders. Complicity may be self-serving, in either survival or fiscal terms; still the enterprise in which one is complicit "goes down" a certain way. Enabling bystanders include persons who suffer from harmful structures, consistent with insights from Marx on false consciousness and ideology, and Bourdieu on symbolic violence. The fact that victims themselves often accept conditions of poverty, inequality, oppression and other injuries as natural and/or acceptable underscores the role of cultural signification in mass harm perhaps most vividly of all.

IDEAS OF HARM

It is axiomatic that our actions are guided by ideas, including all-encompassing worldviews, values, principles, norms, and codes. Our *harmful* actions are guided by ideas that concern who harm victims and agents are and what the nature of harmful practices is. Ideas about who and what is "trouble" guide school discipline, policing, criminal justice policy, and government generally. The impact of profiling or stereotyping on the lives and prospects of individuals and communities is well documented. An ethos of neoliberalism underpins various harm enterprises—overly stringent conditions on public assistance, austerity measures, and limits on global debt relief—to a large extent by assigning responsibility for suffering to victims. The logics of colonialism and gentrification render existing residents of a place invisible and occupation inevitable. The view of a natural moral hierarchy where humans have dominion over nature constructs ecological devastation as consistent with the right order of things.

Criminologists of various stripes explain offending behavior in terms of values and norms, though the behavior in question is usually individual infraction. Hirschi's (1969) social bond theory depicts offenders as adhering more weakly than the rest of us to "beliefs in the moral validity of norms" (p. 26). Social learning theory proposes that we learn "orientations, rationalizations, definitions of the situation, and other attitudes that label the commission of an act as right or wrong, good or bad, desirable or undesirable, justified or unjustified" (Akers 1998, p. 78). Sutherland and Cressey's (1974) formulation of differential association theory, precursor to Akers's social learning theory, proposes that offenders hold "an excess of definitions favorable to violation of law over definitions unfavorable to violation of law" (p. 75). These theories sketch criminogenic beliefs broadly as those that legitimize lawbreaking. Anomie theories, inspired by Durkheim, are concerned with societal values that extol particular versions of success. According to Merton's (1938) anomie (also called strain) theory, when economic success is taken to be a universal end goal but the normative means to achieving such success are not similarly emphasized, individuals who are structurally disadvantaged may turn to crime—to get what they are taught to strive for or to resist the dysfunctional system. Messner and Rosenfeld's (1994) institutional anomie theory holds that the values of the economy, including unfettered competition and individual achievement, in the United States have come to colonize social life, weakening the erstwhile constraining effects of more communitarian and nonpecuniary logics.

Midcentury subcultural criminological theories posited that certain groups, disproportionately young, poor, and male, endorse crime and violence by embracing values such as maliciousness, hedonism, trouble, and excitement (A. Cohen 1955; Miller 1958). The subcultural theorists proposed that delinquents adopt these values after failing in the social mainstream. Matza (1964) and ethnographers such as Anderson (1999) and Bourgois (2003) provide more sophisticated formulations of the notion of group members negotiating, rather than simply holding, subcultural values. Due in part to these more complex explorations, today's criminologists question whether any collective or individual embraces the idea that "harm" generically speaking is "good." Critical criminologists have questioned the supposed normative consensus and prosocial bent of mainstream society, including the notion that "the values of the larger culture contain strong prescriptions for nonviolence" (Wolfgang and Ferracuti 1967, p. 301). Their critiques are both theoretical and empirical—questioning the premise of social homogeneity and highlighting evidence (even celebration) of mainstream brutality and transgression.

In general, analysts of harm concerned with belief systems ask not only what beliefs promote or inhibit harm-doing but also what keeps actors from consistently acting upon those beliefs. In the words of the psychologist Albert Bandura (1999), we need to understand "the mechanisms by which people come to live in accordance with moral standards" (p. 193) and not simply the (abstract) standards themselves. Hence a body of work on how individuals deal with the "cognitive dissonance" of doing harm while opposing it (e.g., Hinton 1996; Lieberman 2006; Maikovich 2005). That those who do harm generally espouse *anti*-harm moral principles and accordingly must dislocate those principles for a time was the grounding idea of Sykes and Matza's (1957) neutralization theory. According to the theory, juvenile delinquency is a function of accounting for it in a particular way prior to acting—by deploying techniques of neutralization, namely, denial of responsibility; denial of injury; denial of the victim; condemnation of the condemners; and appeal to higher loyalties. Connecting neutralization theory to social learning theory, Sykes and Matza propose that neutralizations are learned "'definitions of the situation' which represent tangential or glancing blows at the dominant normative system rather than the creation of an opposing ideology; and they are extensions of patterns of thought prevalent in society rather than something created *de novo*" (1957, p. 669; emphasis in original). The young person subscribes to mainstream edicts against delinquent action but temporarily suspends them.

Moral principles must be suspended because we are emotionally attached to them, and we are emotionally attached to them because our identities are riding on them. The basic point, from learning theory, is that misconduct "will bring self-condemnation" and thus guilt and shame (Bandura 1999, p. 194; see also Braithwaite 1989). That violating our principles has an affective dimension means that the work we do to reconcile our behavior with our principles is affective work, which I entertain further in addressing narrative's exceptionalism (Frank 2010b).

Sykes and Matza (1957) were not especially concerned with mass action. They had in mind individuals, not groups. The individual "feels that his behavior does not really cause any great harm" or "moves himself into the position of avenger" (p. 668) or makes some other ideational adjustment. Although subsequent research framed by neutralization theory has taken heed of mass harm (e.g., Alvarez 1997; Box 1983; S. Cohen 2001), elsewhere neutralizations have been equated with individual-level thinking errors on the part of offenders (Ellis 1973; Yochelson and Samenow 1976). In contrast, a psychology-based literature concerning moral disengagement, a concept that is comparable to neutralization, has been amply applied to mass harm and has stressed that disengagement mechanisms are culturally conditioned, with the lead contribution being that of Bandura (1999; see also Aquina, Reed, Thau, and Freeman 2007; Bandura 1990; Obermann 2011; Petitta, Probst, and Barbaranelli 2015). The means of escaping self-condemnation are not invented by individual minds because we do not reason in isolation. We get our ideas from social sources or "thought communities," which is also the way we learn how to ideologically contravene reigning standards of conduct (Zerubavel 1997). Institutions and institutional norms and laws may set and teach standards of conduct, but they also disseminate acceptable reasons for breaches, as Box (1983) notes concerning corporate crime: "It is not difficult for corporate officials to cover themselves in 'purity' even when they are breaking the law because the 'structural immorality' of their corporate environment provides a library of verbal technique for neutralizing the moral bind of laws against corporate behaviour" (p. 54). The pool of ideas we access has been established as common sense: it has achieved hegemony. The acceptability of those ideas has public sanction and furthermore sustains status quo power positions.

Bandura (1999) proposed four types of moral disengagement that vary by the target of cognitive adjustment:

(a) the reconstrual of the conduct itself so it is not viewed as immoral,
(b) the operation of the agency of action so that the perpetrators can minimize their role in causing harm,
(c) the consequences that flow from actions, or
(d) how the victims of maltreatment are regarded by devaluing them as human beings and blaming them for what is being done to them. (p. 194)

Bandura (1999, p. 204) contends that the mechanisms of moral disengagement work in conjunction with one another, which is well demonstrated in the case of rape myths (Burt 1980; Feild 1978; Schwendinger and Schwendinger 1974). Rape myths, or neutralizations concerning sexual violence, manipulate all four of the targets just mentioned. They are "prejudicial, stereotyped, or false beliefs about rape, rape victims, and rapists" (Burt 1980, p. 217), beliefs such as: many women want to be raped, women can resist rape, some women deserve to be raped, and women often falsely accuse men of rape to get back at them. Burt documented the prevalence of adherence to rape myths and correlated such adherence with more general attitudes about gender (pro-traditional sex roles) and violence (accepting of it) with survey responses to the Rape Myth Acceptance Scale. Of a random sample of nearly six hundred adults in Minnesota surveyed in 1977, for example, more than half agreed with statements such as "In the majority of rapes, the victim is promiscuous or has a bad reputation" (Burt 1980, p. 223). Sexual violence is also promoted by the idea that it does no harm. In this regard Moran (2015) discusses the myths that support prostitution through a powerful accounting of her own experience. These include myths of the prostitute achieving happiness, sexual pleasure, and control through the work. On the question of control Moran writes: "The belief that prostitutes are in control has no basis in reality, but it has two practicable functions, related but distinct: to sanitise and excuse the economic and sexual abuse of women by men, and to obscure the core of prostitution's true nature: the commercialisation of sexual abuse" (pp. 171–72). Prevailing ideas about some system of exploitation disguise and rationalize, with the effect of upholding the power relations that pattern or system supports. It makes sense, then, that the powerful organize *how* we think and *thereby* what we think.

Herbert Kelman (1973) theorizes institutional sway over cognition in a morally extreme action context—that of massacring innocents. Kelman first refutes individual explanations. He notes that psychologically normal people are seen to perpetrate this kind of violence. Nor, in his view, do emotions such as frustration and hostility motivate such violence, though they often accompany it. For Kelman anger and sadism are not "major motivating forces in their own right" (p. 36) but at best facilitators and even outcomes of the actual causal factors, which are conditions that weaken erstwhile moral restraints against violence. Such weakening is the result of three social processes—authorization, routinization, and dehumanization: "Through processes of authorization, the situation becomes so defined that standard moral principles do not apply and the individual is absolved of responsibility to make personal moral choices. Through processes of routinization, the action becomes so organized that there is no opportunity for raising moral questions and making moral decisions. Through processes of dehumanization, the actor's attitudes toward the target and toward himself become so structured that it is neither necessary nor possible for him to view the relationship in moral terms" (p. 38). Although Kelman scarcely refers to cognition per se, the three morality-attenuating processes that he identifies operate cognitively. Authorization and dehumanization lead us to invest in particular definitions of the situation, self and target, for example, a view of compulsion by (or paramount loyalty toward) authorities, and the idea that the victim is not part of the human community.[3] Authorization can also work more subtly and more pervasively when authoritarian regimes cast doubt on facts and the media that disseminate them; in this way the government delegitimizes potentially contradictory ideas. Routinization, like bureaucratization, is a material process, "transforming the action into routine, mechanical, highly programmed operations" (Kelman 1973, p. 46). Kelman's theory echoes Arendt's (1963) "banality of evil thesis" according to which the Nazi regime transformed people carrying out the genocide into "functionaries and mere cogs" (p. 289). Routinization operates via ideas in the sense that it helps actors avoid contemplating what they are doing or the outcomes they are contributing to: "Routinization fulfills two functions. First, it reduces the necessity of making decisions, thus minimizing occasions in which moral questions may arise. Second, it makes it easier to avoid the implications of the action since the actor focuses on the details of his job rather than on its meaning" (Kelman 1973, p. 46). Kelman's moral actor is situated to think certain things and, more important, not to think others. Not thinking about the ethics of one's actions—or inactions—is highly consequential and wholly socialized. Thus, too, Bandura (1999) refers to "decisional arrangements of foggy nonresponsibility" where "authorities act in ways that keep themselves intentionally uninformed" (p. 197). These arrangements insulate actors from sanction in the event that harm is publicized, as well as self-sanction, for these actors "also have to live with themselves" (p. 197).

Not thinking about what one is doing brings us to habit and Bourdieu's (1977) concept of habitus, "a system of lasting, transposable dispositions which, integrating past experiences, functions at every moment as a *matrix of perceptions, appreciations, and actions*" (pp. 82–83; emphasis in original). Perception, appreciation, and action are enmeshed in this perspective. Habitus is embodied, something on the order of playbook moves, not *necessarily* thought of yet reciprocally related to ideas as well as other structures. Discursive forms are among the structures that inculcate and reflect habitus (see Fleetwood 2016).

DISCURSIVE FORMS

Ideas and mechanisms that manipulate ideas and thinking are made concrete and disseminated through semiotic processes. Messages of harm's legitimacy are embodied in particular statements. For example, boys' routine violence lends itself to a popular figure of speech called an *epanelepsis*: "Boys will be boys." Is it significant that the normalization of boys' violence is captured in *discourse*? In other words, does discursivity have a unique impact?

The answer from many quarters is yes. Philosophers and psychologists have advanced a variety of theses to the effect that language constitutes thought. Carruthers (2002) observes that the weakest of these, that "language makes some cognitive difference" (p. 659), enjoys broad support. Yet, he gathers evidence for the stronger claim that language is a *necessary* medium of thought across domains. Language both integrates and communicates ideas, whereas other "modules" such as the visual do not.

That is, language "has both input and output functions" (p. 666). We make the world meaningful to ourselves and to others through language.

But texts do not merely clarify; they also make things happen (Austin 1962). Or, as Barthes (1957) says of myth, "It makes us understand something and it imposes it on us" (p. 117). Texts establish positions and institutions. Even where the ideas that inspired them are not consciously received or even accepted, discourses govern through the hierarchies they construct. Thus, van Dijk (1992) takes note of the discursive strategies with which racialized hierarchies are maintained. Where overtly racist expressions are inconsistent with prevailing norms, whites use strategies like reversal, where "anti-racists tend to be represented as the ones who are intolerant" (van Dijk 1992, p. 94). Van Dijk (1993) situates the role of language this way: "A discourse analytical approach does not imply that we reduce the problem of racism to a language or communication problem. Obviously, racism also manifests itself in many non-discursive practices and structures, such as discrimination in employment, housing, health care, and social services, or in physical aggression. Our major claim and interest, then, are twofold: (1) Racism also manifests itself in discourse and communication, often in relation with other social practices of oppression and exclusion, and (2) the social cognitions that underlie these practices are largely shaped through discursive communication within the dominant white group" (p. 13). Here, discourse both reflects and molds thought. The idea of that reciprocal relation is compatible with Foucault's (2000) perspective on the political impact of ideas *as* discourses, which flow from particular "regimes of truth." Among discourses I distinguish between what I call *wording* and *narrative*.

Wording

By *wording* I mean to demarcate linguistic processes that are more or less contained in a few words and whose use is relatively flexible across statements. They may amount to systems, but it is useful to focus attention on distinct devices—words or groups of words.[4] For example, we find across harms the negative labeling of targets: "The use of labels helps to deprive the victims of identity and community. Terms like 'gook' help to define them as subhuman, despicable, and certainly incapable of evoking empathy. Terms like 'Communist' allow their total identity to be absorbed by a single category, and one that is identified by the perpetrators of the massacre as totally evil" (Kelman 1973, p. 50).

Not just labels, but labeling schemes—classifications, or "differentiations" (Lévi-Strauss 1966)—are a vital aspect of the enculturation of harm. A raft of studies has turned up classificatory systems that are essential to war, colonialism, slavery, prostitution, and more, distinguishing, for example, virgin and whore, ruler and subject, Occidental and Oriental, and master and slave. Abortion is opposed by reference to "killing babies" (Lakoff 2002). The sharp distinction between victims and offenders, however those roles are cast, is essential to punishment schemes. Yet, harm-promoting classifications are not necessarily binary, illustrated by Lombroso's (1876) typology of criminals (e.g., the born criminal, criminaloids, the criminal by passion, and others) and South Africa's rule of apartheid (black, white, Coloured, and Indian).

The harm-inducing effects of labels that pertain to deviance and criminality are central to the labeling perspective in sociology. The labeling perspective applies to mass harm to the extent that it concerns itself with groups and definitions of crime that criminalize them, following conflict theory (see, e.g., Quinney 1970). The labeling of target groups facilitates their mistreatment. Numerous studies have inventoried figurative expressions for victims of mass harm. In particular, much has been written about the dehumanizing terms that genocide perpetrators use to refer to their victims (e.g., Alvarez 1997; Bélanger-Vincent 2009; Fox and Levin 1998; Hagan and Rymond-Richmond 2008; Huggins, Haritos-Fatouros, and Zimbardo 2002; cf. Williams and Neilsen 2016). Haslam (2006) usefully conceptualizes dehumanization as attributing to others *either* animalistic *or* object-like qualities, thus opening up the (latter) possibility of objective and equable dehumanization that takes "everyday forms" (p. 255). I have shown that harm projects in general rely on reductive but not necessarily animallike or debasing constructions of harm targets (Presser 2013).[5]

Discourse also permits concealment. "Defense of marriage" legislation in the United States shrouds discrimination against gay people, and "right to work" laws are designed to combat unionization. Communication scholar Walter Fisher (1987) finds "code words" in the speech of Ronald Reagan during his run for the U.S. presidency: "'[F]amily' means the nuclear family—dad, mom, son, and daughter; 'neighborhood' means no busing; 'work' means no welfare but 'work-fare'; 'peace' means the United States must be the biggest, strongest country in the world in order that we preserve the peace and fulfill our manifest destiny to spread our way of life everywhere. 'Freedom' means freedom from governmental interference in the 'free-enterprise' system" (p. 151). Orwell (1968) said of political discourse generally that it is "designed to make lies sound truthful and murder respectable" (p. 139) and "largely the defence of the indefensible" (p. 136). Often, though not always, harm projects—or the harmful aspects of a practice—must be obscured if they are to meet with general tolerance, hence the use of euphemism as well as outright denial. Denial may be hard to render credible (and requires tampering with records, disappearing victims, and so forth), so euphemism would seem to be more common. Of the mass murder of Jews by the Nazis, Arendt (1963) explains: "All correspondence referring to [the mass killing of Jews] was subject to rigid 'language rules,' and, except in the reports from the *Einsatzgruppen* [mobile units of shooters], it is rare to find documents in which such bald words as 'extermination,' 'liquidation,' or 'killing' occur. The prescribed code names for killing were 'final solution,' 'evacuation' *(Aussiedlung)*, and 'special treatment' *(Sonderbehandlung)*; ... Moreover, the very term 'language rule' *(Sprachregelung)* was itself a code name; it meant what in ordinary language would be called a lie" (p. 85). Language rules facilitated the cloaking of reality such that harm agents were able to delude themselves and others as to what they were really doing. Even the delusions were represented euphemistically: speakers lied to themselves about the fact of lying. That they spoke in code meant a subterfuge for their actions, to the outside world and to themselves.

Coding is surely culturally and historically specific. "Final solution" was typical of the ethos of technocratic problem solving promoted by the Nazi regime. Today, neoliberalism frames many harmful actions and patterns as positive in part by constructing them as sites of choice in a marketplace of options. Hence, celebrations of "diversity" provide cover for social inequalities and even render racial difference "the source of brand value" (Gray 2013, p. 771). "School choice" (Douglas-Gabriel and Jan 2017) and "justice campuses" (Schept 2015) prompt notions of people with options and thereby efface oppression, inequality, and hardship.

Some of the most careful elaborations of the impact of linguistic figuration on mass harm are feminist works. These stress misrepresentation and obfuscation via prevailing expressions for gendered harming and harm victims. They also show that societal relations of power enable certain discourses to achieve hegemony and thereupon solidify those relations of power. For example, Beneke (1982) undertook a study of rape-enabling metaphors that reaffirms Burt's (1980) study of rape myths, discussed previously, but attends more closely to discourse. What Beneke (1982) calls *rape language*, discerned through interviews with men, includes the following metaphors:

- Sex is achievement.
- Sex is a commodity.
- Sex is possession.
- Sex is madness.
- Women are objects.
- A woman's appearance is a weapon.
- Rape is theft of a valued commodity.
- Rape is instruction.

These metaphors have impactful variants, such as sex is a particular kind of achievement like a game or a war.

Planning for harm is likewise configured through gendered metaphors. Cohn (1987) describes metaphors in use that link nuclear planning to sexuality (e.g., a weapon producing "an orgasmic whump"); virginity (e.g., a bomb "losing her virginity"); domesticity (e.g., "weapons systems can 'marry up'") and prosocial interaction more generally (e.g., "pat a B-1"), birth (e.g., "It's a boy"); and godliness (e.g., "the nuclear priesthood"). Cohn (1987) summarizes:

> Language that is abstract, sanitized, full of euphemisms; language that is sexy and fun to use; paradigms whose referent is weapons; imagery that domesticates and deflates the forces of mass destruction; imagery that reverses sentient and nonsentient matter, that conflates birth and death, destruction and creation—all of these are part of what makes it possible to be radically removed from the reality of what one is talking about and from the realities one is creating through the discourse. *Learning to speak* the language reveals something about how thinking can become more abstract, more focused on parts disembedded from their context, more attentive to the survival of weapons than the survival of human beings. (p. 715; emphasis in original)

Language demarcates thought and speech, disallowing "certain questions to be asked or certain values to be expressed" (Cohn 1987, p. 708) and thus governing what can be contemplated and debated. The language of defense planning, Cohn discovered, precludes a holistic perspective on what people are truly up to: "The problem ... is not only that the language is narrow but also that it is seen by its speakers as complete or whole unto itself—as representing a body of truths that exist independently of any other truth or knowledge" (p. 712). The "technostrategic discourse" Cohn was privy to acts "as an ideological curtain behind which the actual reasons for these (nuclear weapons development and deployment) decisions hide.... rather than informing and shaping decisions, it far more often functions as a legitimation for political outcomes that have occurred for utterly different reasons" (p. 716). The discourse obscures reality.

Similarly, in *The Sexual Politics of Meat*, Carol Adams (1990) emphasizes wording and the concealment it effects. She juxtaposes violence against nonhumans with violence against women in order to demonstrate that "patriarchal culture authorizes the eating of animals" (p. 13). She points out ways in which the oppression of women and nonhuman animals is conjointly accomplished, and feminist vegetarian resistance defused, through discourse. First, the experience, even the beingness, of nonhuman animals and women goes missing in the mainstream language of patriarchal societies (p. 40): "Just as dead bodies are absent from our language about meat, in descriptions of cultural violence women are also often the absent referent. Rape, in particular, carries such potent imagery that the term is transferred from the literal experience of women and applied metaphorically to other instances of violent devastation, such as the 'rape' of the earth in ecological writings of the early 1970s" (pp. 42–43). As such, language distances us from the "literal facts" (p. 75) of experiences of violence. Second, the relatedness of male to female and human to nonhuman is denied through various discursive means—by representing "man" as the universal human, using "animal" for nonhuman animal and thus denying that humans are animals as well, using the degendered "it" for nonhumans, and using metaphors that regularize violence toward nonhumans (e.g., "beating a dead horse") (pp. 64–65). Third, animal bodies that are killed for meat are largely female or feminized bodies: "We oppress animals by associating them with women's lesser status" (p. 72). Fourth, women and nonhumans are assigned to one of two mutually exclusive subject positions: "good or evil, emblems of divine perfection or diabolical incarnations, Mary or Eve, pet or beast" (p. 74). Adams refers to such classification in binary moral terms as "false naming" (p. 74). Overall, Adams exposes untruths about nonhuman animals and women, the telling of which linguistic representations facilitate.

Arran Stibbe (2001) covers some of the same ground as Adams, undertaking a critical discourse analysis of the syntaxes, idioms, metaphors, and other features of the language disseminated by meat industries concerning nonhuman animals and their treatment. For example, nonhuman animals are referred to in volume rather than count terms, thus erasing their individuality. Metaphors treat animals (e.g., breeding sows) as machinery and other things "to encourage the disregard of animal suffering" (Stibbe 2001, p. 156). Notably, Stibbe's data are drawn from professional journals and industry publications, which have the reputation of conveying facts literally.

Generally speaking, figurativeness functions as a kind of subterfuge in the foregoing studies. The focus on language for deception hones a view of language as shaping perception to the exclusion of emotion. However, language shapes not just how we think but also what we feel. Further, the focus on language for deception implies strategy. It should be remembered, though, that bad faith is not a necessary aspect of the power of language to shape our view of things.[6] No one need *intend* to manipulate or conceal.

The issue of manipulation brings us to ideology and propaganda, which lack the concreteness of ideas *and* wording (as well as narrative). They are essentially hybrid forms. Propaganda pertains to discourse but is centrally a matter of manipulating beliefs. Stanley (2015) defines political propaganda as "a kind of speech that fundamentally involves political, economic, aesthetic, or rational ideals, mobilized for a political purpose" (p. 52). The form that propaganda may take is open. Ideology is even less tangible. Eagleton (1991) points out that ideology has numerous definitions, including ones that are politics-neutral, such as "action-oriented sets of beliefs" (p. 2); ones that are less neutral, such as "the forms of thought motivated by social interests" (p. 1); and ones that highlight discourse over belief, such as "the points where power impacts upon certain utterances and inscribes itself tacitly within them" (p. 223). We can call ideas, wording, *or* narratives ideological if they construct or maintain hierarchies and harms. And we can think about the impact of propaganda or ideology that is structured narratively.

Narrative

Narrative, we have seen, is a discursive form that meaningfully recounts some experience. Some of the aforementioned studies of discourse in mass harm engage the concept of narrative, usually sparingly or obliquely. The overarching "themes" that inform pro-rape metaphors in Beneke's (1982) analysis are narratives in abbreviated form. For example, the theme that men are victims of women's sexual attractiveness reflects a simple plot: women arouse men, men become helpless. It is a victimization *story.* Adams (1990) observes that the slaughter of nonhuman animals is rooted in basic expectations of a "story of meat": "The birth of an animal and the beginning of the story lock the story in a traditional movement of narrativity and a cultural one of reciprocity. We give them life and later can take it, precisely because in the beginning we gave it. Based on our knowledge of how the story is going to end we interpret its beginning" (p. 93). Adams is pointing to a basic narrative of the ontology of nonhumans, with an emphasis on requisite events in a certain order.

That story of meat is reminiscent of stories of other harms in the present day according to which victims are blamed because they get what they asked for, were paid for, or deserve: think police brutality against youth who are allegedly disrespectful or delinquent, or the degradation of prostitutes who are paid to endure it. Each case involves a storied exchange; each connects to a neoliberal logic that can be summed up with the phrase "you bought in" (or "you knew the score") or, for the most degraded targets such as nonhumans and slaves, "you were sold." Very different but no less harmful are euphemistic narratives, such as narratives of racial progress at home and humanitarian good in the world, whose message is "there is no problem here." They mute outrage and activism and obscure what causes misery and remains to be challenged (Kendi 2017).

By its focus on narrative as the paramount discursive engine of harm, narrative criminology entails a more systematic and thick analysis of narratives than the studies just discussed. Narrative criminologists are analysts, who closely attend to plots and the characters that carry the plots along.

Carol Mason (2002) studied antiabortion violence in the United States through pro-life writings from the 1960s to the turn of the twenty-first century. She paid special attention to the 1990s when violence against abortion clinics and providers peaked. She found that an apocalyptic narrative "gives ideological coherence" (p. 2) to the pro-life position, uniting mainstream and extremist adherents. The narrative constructs "some particular people as pro-life warriors and others as conspiratorial enemies of life" (p. 191): "Narrating the new abortion warrior as besieged, outnumbered, and victimized, pro-life writing makes the white, Christian, heterosexual (and working- or middle-class) male a hero above all others. Despite the fact that people, regardless of their race, gender, sexuality, religion, class, or ethnicity, may deplore abortion and fashion sophisticated reasons to prohibit it, pro-life ideology habitually and consistently defines its hero as male, straight, Christian, and white" (p. 190). Adversaries in the narrative are Jewish, African American, or immigrant physicians who get rich from abortions and lesbian nurses who take depraved pleasure in performing them. The innocent unborn are likewise racialized and gendered: they are typically evoked as male and white and abortion is depicted as "the end times of the white race" (p. 98). Mason contends that fetuses are "proxy victims" for "the psychological and political abuses some men believe they have experienced in the wake of social change since the 1960s" (p. 193). The apocalyptic narrative reinstates waning white male power. Whereas in the research of Cohn (1987) and Adams (1990) reviewed earlier, elite discourse affirms the patriarchal order, in Mason's (2002) more historically attentive study of subcultural illicit violence, (narrative) discourse recovers that order. It looks backward to better times (for white men) and forward to the ultimate triumph through social metamorphosis. Hence "the principle behind killing for life is not the sanctity of life but the apocalyptic prophecy of millennialism" (Mason 2002, p. 72).

Another important illustration of narrative guiding mass harm takes us to the cultural center of societies. In *Why War?* Philip Smith (2005) identifies the narrative genres with which three international political conflicts implicating the United States—the Suez Crisis, the Persian Gulf War, and the Iraq War—were framed in the media and by political officials: low mimesis, tragedy, romance, and apocalyptic. He finds: "When successfully institutionalized and widely shared the apocalyptic frame encourages war" (P. Smith 2005, p. 205). In contrast: "Realist and tragic frames are associated with low levels of legitimacy and military intervention" (p. 205). The realist or low mimetic genre orients to instrumentality and thus lacks drama; romance emphasizes the potential for transformation by interpersonal means; and tragedy inspires inaction out of a pessimistic sense of futility. The apocalyptic narrative "involves the most intense character polarization that involves the highest and lowest of human motivations" (p. 26). Given its intensity, to tell an apocalyptic narrative is to engage in "narrative inflation," as seen in American civil discourses in August 1990, some months prior to the start of the Persian Gulf War: "Narrative inflation set in with powers of action becoming more awe-inspiring, objects of struggle more global and less local, and motivations for action less routine, less rationally accountable and more maniacal, more diabolical" (p. 105). Narrative deflation is also possible, "downgrading the object of struggle and reducing the narrative polarization between the protagonists" (p. 82). Smith thus emphasizes the dynamism involved in deploying narrative genres.

When a crisis mounts, we do not so much declare a genre as "guess" at one. "Citizens, journalists, commentators, and politicians take prior knowledge and the bits and pieces of information at hand and then, to put them together into a meaningful whole, each makes their genre guess" (P. Smith 2005, pp. 31–32). What follows is "a dialogue about validity" (p. 32), potentially culminating in "a genre war" (p. 32). The business of designating a narrative genre is prone to struggle because the stakes are high. Whether mass harm is waged depends on the genre that gains official acceptance.

Like Smith, Patrick Colm Hogan (2006) is concerned with narratives of the nation in (alleged) trouble. Hogan similarly deals in narrative genres—calling them *prototypes*—but also highlights the collective cognitions, experiences, concerns, and cultural artifacts that would direct the populace toward one prototype over another. German nationalism after World War I could have taken a few narrative forms, and indeed, the "heroic narrative" is nationalism's default narrative prototype in general (see Hogan 2003). However, Germany had suffered tremendous defeat (during and in the aftermath of the Great War) and collective devastation, experiences that are associated with a sacrificial narrative, not a heroic one. The Nazi version of the "sacrificial narrative" prototype sought "to end devastation by sacrificing members of the out-group blamed for entering into and destroying the home society" (Hogan 2006, p. 94). The main out-group would be the Jews. Hogan explicates one mass media shaper of that prototype in the form of F.W. Murnau's acclaimed horror film *Nosferatu: A Symphony of Horror*, which premiered in Germany in 1922. The film depicts a naive and virtuous German couple, a plague-ridden and evil outsider, and an "initial crime for which the entire society will suffer" (p. 103)—German greed and ignorance leading to collaboration with the diseased and degenerate enemy, whom visual cues establish as Jewish. Hogan maintains that this popular plotline helped set the stage for Nazi violence: "Films such as *Nosferatu*—along with novels, plays, political speeches, ordinary discourse—helped to orient and specify the way German people thought about nationalism in the interwar years. Audience members necessarily linked the events and characters of the film with pre-existing prototypes (e.g., regarding Jews or immigration). Moreover, they tacitly drew these connections in the context of persistent anxieties regarding the devastation of their society, anxieties that were already likely to prime a sacrificial prototype" (p. 104). *Nosferatu* served to "prime links between the sacrificial structure and stereotypes of Jews, as well as thoughts about infection, memories of national devastation, and so forth" (p. 95). The film helped cement those represented linkages in the collective consciousness.

Robert M. Keeton (2015) analyzed atrocities against Native Americans in terms of Old Testament narratives, specifically, the creation story from the book of Genesis, the story of the exodus of the Israelites from bondage in Egypt, and the story of Jacob and Esau, as these were cited in congressional debates, popular essays, and political correspondence. The Indian Removal Act of 1830 resulted in the relocation of Native American people, resulting in the destruction of lives and tribal cultures. Biblical narratives were used to reduce the social status of the Native people and legitimize their exile to the West. America was "the New Israel" or Promised Land that God promised to his preferred children: "During the Indian removal debate, the primary function of the Jacob and Esau narrative was to provide a moral justification for placing the agricultural lifestyle of Western Europeans above the hunter-gatherer lifestyle of indigenous tribes in America. Jacob was the symbol of white agrarian society and Esau represented the 'red' man, the nomadic hunter who was destined to lose his birthright to those who would fulfill God's mandate to till the soil" (Keeton 2015, p. 140). Biblical narratives set out plots and assigned characters, as do all narratives, the distinction here being the consecration of these plots and character assignments by God.

Likewise attuned to religious forms, Halverson, Goodall, and Corman (2011) identified thirteen "master narratives" channeled by Islamist extremists to incite terrorist acts. Mobilization, in their view, involves drawing analogies between present conditions and one or more of the master narratives. "In Islamist discourse, the known situations are those described in the stories of the master narratives, and the strategic objective is to establish similarities between them and current events" (p. 191). A master narrative invokes one or more "story forms," which Halverson, Goodall, and Corman (2011) define as "generic frameworks ... identifying the entities (usually, but not necessarily people) that are involved, the actions they take, and how these actions relate to one another" (p. 184). Examples of story forms are deliverance, betrayal, invasion, and noble sacrifice: "The Tart master narrative alone contains no less than three story forms with accompanying archetypes in its various components; however, the principal story form is invasion. This sort of internal complexity and variety makes these master narratives particularly useful for framing a range of events and circumstances and helps to ensure their cultural longevity and persistence among extremists seeking to persuade Muslim audiences" (p. 124).

Halverson and colleagues point out that a message of destiny/necessity and the breadth of potential application help account for narrative power. On the one hand, as in Hogan's work on the Holocaust, the mechanisms are cognitive. Master narratives "convince" audiences and "naturalize" ideas (Halverson, Goodall, and Corman 2011, p. 195). They help people "understand their roles, duties, and goals" (p. 201). On the other hand, the narratives have an invitational edge not altogether captured by ideation. Like Smith referring to the subjunctive mood of narrative, Halverson and colleagues stress the seduction of what the hero could but might not make happen: "It is important to note ... that while all story forms have a preferred outcome—the satisfaction of the desire rooted in conflict—that these desired endings *do not always occur.* In fact, the allure of a preferred ending is a powerful inducement to do whatever work is required to bring it about" (p. 21; emphasis in original). Some narratives are more precarious than others. For example, the Nakba and Mahdi master narratives are unfinished in that "the rescuer has yet to come along" (pp. 186–87): they "cry out for a rescuer to emerge on the scene" (p. 187). The heady role of rescuer is established, but it has yet to be cast.

Sandberg (2013) is also concerned with how would-be terrorists cast themselves. His study of Norwegian terrorist Anders Behring Breivik, based on a fifteen-hundred-page treatise Breivik wrote and distributed widely via e-mail just before his attacks, highlights the "creativity and artfulness" (p. 79) of Breivik's storied self-constructions—variously, as professional revolutionary, evangelist, pragmatic conservative, and sociable/likable person.[7] "The terrorist attacks in Norway were enactments of a particular set of political narratives" beset by contradictions (p. 80). Again we find precariousness, here a sort of hedging as to who one essentially is. Narrative creativity allows the narrator to broaden the appeal of his discursive project.

In *Why We Harm* (Presser 2013) I collapsed boundaries between harmful actions to develop a general narrative logic of harm. Using a variety of materials including data from semistructured interviews, I studied ways that people talk about intimate partner violence, genocide, criminal punishment, and meat eating. The logic of harm, I found, consists in a reduction of who the target is (e.g., "slut" or "meat"), as well as an internally contradictory rhetoric concerning one's power to act harmfully *and* inability to act otherwise: "Harm agents project both power and powerlessness" (p. 117). I termed this discursive maneuver a *power paradox*, "a radical, discursive expression of the human condition" (p. 118) but amplified in the harm context. For example, we demand violence against the enemy, highlighting purpose and resolve even as the action is purportedly preordained, a fated next step in the people's progress. An additional harm-promoting discursive maneuver is the reduction of harm targets. As I mentioned earlier in this chapter, to reduce one's targets is to characterize them in terms of very few interests, or to characterize them as having few interests that are distinct from what one has in mind for them. The former is most relevant to the harm we cause humans; the latter is most often seen in cases of harm to nonhumans like other animals and the planet.

Across harms, with the exception of meat eating, I found that the logic of harm took the form of stories—of protagonists moving forward in time, negotiating meaningful conflicts with an eye toward some future (Presser 2013). Most of the meat eaters interviewed for the study eschewed the need to *tell* a story altogether. The story of meat is pervasive in our cultural environment; it seems not to warrant individual expression. Nonetheless, the story has been and gets told. Nonhuman animals are cast as "meat" with few interests. We have every right to their flesh and at the same time can barely help but partake. How does the story of meat affect us *beyond* the question of its permissibility or impermissibility? In other words, how does it make us *feel*? A look at narrative's exceptionalism can help address that question.

NARRATIVE EXCEPTIONALISM

Narrative is a uniquely affecting cultural form. Three bases for its exceptionalism can be sketched at this point, to be expanded on in the next chapter. Before turning to these bases for narrative exceptionalism, it is necessary to review what I would call regular features of narrative: *temporality*, *causality*, *action*, *conflict*, *transformation*, *meaning*, and *situatedness*. One can find narratives without one or more of these features—say, a narrative without any conflict, in which case the "narrativity" (D. Herman 2002) or "storyness" (Hogan 2003) of the text is diminished. Nonetheless, these regular features of narrative are amply discussed in the narrative literature, and they help audiences to recognize a narrative *as* a narrative. They are related to one another, as will become clear, but are distinguished here for exposition. In addition to those seven regular features, I discuss an eighth feature, less often addressed in narrative studies generally but vital for narrative impact, that of leaving *things unsaid.*

Temporality

A narrative is widely considered to be a time-ordered progression of experiences. Ricoeur (1984) is well known for proposing that narratives are about time passing *and* that we experience time passing in narrative terms. In other words, time and narrative are reciprocally related. That relation is vivid in the context of histories, both collective and personal. Kermode (1967) explains the psychological need for the temporality of life stories: "For to make sense of our lives from where we are, as it were, stranded in the middle, we need fictions of beginnings and fictions of ends, fictions which unite beginning and end and endow the interval between them with meaning" (p. 190). Stereotypical fairy tales begin and end with time references ("Once upon a time"; "They lived happily ever after"), and one assumes that the in-between is a chronological middle. Even stories told "out of order," such as through flashback, reflect the passing of time in the *fabula*, or realm of alleged experience.[8]

Causality

Narratives do not merely register successive experiences: they relate them as causes and effects. Or, to use George Wilson's (2003) fine words, narratives "are thick with causal claims" (p. 403). Romeo kills himself *because* he believes that Juliet is dead. Goldilocks jumps out of the window *because* the three bears return home. Currie (2010) calls narratives "artefactual representations which emphasize the causal and temporal connectedness of particular things, especially agents" (p. 219). Frank (2010a) captures narrative as "one thing happens in consequence of another" (p. 25). Narrative answers the question "Why?" It gives explanations for events, actions, and their sequencing. Accordingly, we tend to tell stories when we are held accountable for something we have done. To quote Charles Tilly (2006): "When most people take reasons seriously, those reasons arrive in the form of stories" (p. 95).

Action

For most narrative analysts, narratives relate what persons do and do intentionally. Hence Burke's (1945) pentad of stories consists of act, scene, agent, agency, and purpose. A story without action—just experiences, perhaps—is hardly imaginable: at least some characters must be agents. "Actions appear so central to narrative that theorists often summarize narratives in terms of their actions alone," Altman (2008, p. 11) observes. In addition, narratives may refer to what was *not* done—"roads not taken" that Prince (1992) incorporates into the category of "disnarrated" material.

Conflict

Along with agency, narratives are said to depend on "surprises or coincidences or encounters or recognition scenes" (Ricoeur 1984, p. 150), a "breach between ideal and real, self and society" (Riessman 1993, p. 3), a "complicating action" (Labov 1972, p. 363), or *peripeteia* (Aristotle 1996). Freytag's (1895) pyramid of drama elaborates the precursors and consequences of the conflict, consisting in exposition, rising action, climax, falling action, and resolution and denouement. Across theories of narrative, scholars largely agree on a standard story pattern of "complication, crisis, and resolution" (Gottschall 2012, p. 54). Hence David Herman's (2002) observation: "A minimal condition for narrative can be defined as the thwarting of intended actions by unplanned, sometimes unplannable, events, which may or may not be the effect of other participants' intended actions. This is another way of expressing the intuition that stories prototypically involve *conflict*, or some sort of (noteworthy, tellable) disruption of an internal state of equilibrium by an unplanned and often untoward event or chain of events" (p. 84; emphasis in original).

Conflict is a phenomenon that only social actors, including the narrator and the narrator's interlocutors, can determine in a given case. Whatever is routine or status quo, given cultural designations, is *not* the usual stuff of stories. Instead, stories tend to focus "attention on the unusual and the remarkable against a backdrop made up of highly structured patterns of belief and expectation" (D. Herman 2002, p. 90). That narrative has long had "precious little use for the simple, calm, and happy" (Brooks 1984, p. 155) gives clues as to why we seem hardly to react to hegemonic stories of institutionalized harm, which have been assimilated into the culture and thus stripped of drama, about which more later.

Transformation

Something is transformed as a result of the narrated conflict. Todorov (1977) describes the "minimal complete plot" as consisting in "the passage from one equilibrium to another" (p. 111), the fullest version consisting in a shift from some equilibrium to disequilibrium to a new equilibrium. The transformation is presumed to be caused by earlier events and actions (Forster 1927). In advance of systematic exploration of the emotional undertow exerted by narrative, I would suggest provisionally that a pattern with the most extreme reversals is likely to be the most powerful (Nabi and Green 2015).

Meaning

A narrative is expected to make a point. It "ceaselessly substitutes meaning for the straightforward copy of the events recounted" (Barthes 1977, p. 119). According to Todorov (1977), "The *perspectivism* proper to narrative cannot be 'reduced,' it constitutes, on the contrary, one of narrative's most important characteristics" (p. 223; emphasis in original). The weightiest stories make points that are generalizable, usually having to do with right living—that is, with morality.[9] Labov (1972) treats evaluation as a discrete structural element of the narrative. Other scholars find it threaded through the text (e.g., De Fina and Georgakopoulou 2012) and emphasize its inconspicuousness. Thus Harold (2005) observes: "Even highly moralistic fiction seeks to demonstrate moral claims indirectly by showing, not stating, that things turn out well when one acts in a certain way, and not otherwise" (p. 176).

Self-narratives make a point concerning *who one is*.[10] Hence an influential view from narrative psychology, that we identify ourselves via our biographical stories (Linde 1993; McAdams 1999; Polonoff 1987; Rosenwald and Ochberg 1992; Sarbin 1986).[11] We set out a stabilizing "what we are like" through "our" stories.

Yet, our self-narratives, and thus our identities, are works in progress that clearly change with new experiences, discursive resources, and interlocutors.

Situatedness

Narratives are socially situated. They are tailored to the (e.g., institutional) circumstances of telling, particular interlocutors, and cultural contexts (Presser 2004, 2005). Thus, no once-and-for-all narrative exists. David Herman (2009) notes that "even in the case of stories not told to others, narratives are shaped by the sociocommunicative environment in which they are produced" (p. 17). I might relate the story of the Fall from Genesis 3, in which Eve's transgression dooms Adam and everyone else, in an article for a feminist journal, in which case my point concerns the representation of women. Inside of a church, the "same" story makes other points. Different reasons for telling the story lead to the production of different stories.

A narrative is also always situated in a field of other narratives, connecting and responding to these others; as Polletta (2006) notes, "Plot depends on previous plots" (p. 169). Earlier stories provide context as well as license and credibility to later stories and storytellers. Stories may rouse us because they link to other stories we retain in "inner libraries," to use Frank's useful concept. Conversely, a story might not "resonate with any inner story" (Frank 2010a, p. 62), in which case it makes little impression on us.

Things Unsaid

Earlier I discussed oblique communication of meaning. On a related note, things go unsaid in narrative. Narratives are highly selective and must be if they are to hone a point, about experience and beings, and not go on endlessly. Hayden White (1980) observes that "every narrative, however seemingly 'full,' is constructed on the basis of a set of events which *might have been included but were left out*; and this is as true of imaginary as it is of realistic narratives" (p. 14; emphasis in original). Content that the narrator, taking cues from culture, deems trivial, unnecessary to mention or unmentionable, is omitted (Prince 1992). Secondhand stories are told in a way that is attuned to new demands of the telling. Although absences receive limited attention in both social and literary research (methodological badlands that absences are), they are a key aspect of narrative's invitational edge. Recipients of the underwritten narrative are more involved than they would be if the narrative were, theoretically, more complete. Iser (1972) states that "it is only through inevitable omissions that a story will gain its dynamism" (p. 284). Relatedly, it is precisely because one's self-narrative at any point is underwritten that the narrator is able to adapt it to new events and understandings.

The review just completed of narrative's regular features—temporality, causality, action, conflict, transformation, meaning, situatedness, and things unsaid—puts us in a position to reflect on what makes narratives uniquely powerful.

First, narratives alone set out an *integrated common sense of action.* Cue temporality, causality, and action. A deeper and more criminologically relevant way of understanding this integrative function returns us to Bandura's (1999) mechanisms of moral disengagement. Narratives potentially engage all four of the mechanisms he identifies—those that target action itself, agency of action, consequences of action, and victims (Bandura 1999). These form a gestalt within narratives. One can imagine, for instance, a story of the decent citizen standing by (agency) while politicians enact a travel policy (action) that causes "inconvenience" (consequences) to "illegals" (victims). The story links characterizations of persons, agency, and action. Even where one of these is underdeveloped (recall things unsaid), the story nonetheless suggests some sort of pattern. It creates that pattern out of persons, events, and experiences.

Second, narratives are about *dynamic agency.* By design, and unique among discursive forms, they account for shifts in circumstances and, accordingly, changes in our capacity to control the circumstances of our lives. The vagaries of our power in narrative bear a likeness to the vagaries of our power in lived experience. The archetype of the narrative where agency is in flux is the morality tale or apocalyptic account of injustice, crisis, and ruin (see, e.g., Fantasia and Hirsch 2003; Gamson, Fireman, and Rytina 1982; Oberschall 2000; P. Smith 2005). Such tales reach their apotheosis when power is restored. And so we can say that narratives also have the potential to shut down dynamic agency, in which case the end of the story provides sought-over closure.

Third, to narrate is to *explain and therefore to moralize* (H. White 1980). Narratives explicate motivated conduct. Characters act with purpose in a world where action affects others. Frank (2010b) puts it neatly: "Without stories there would be no sense of action as ethical" (p. 665). In contrast, ideas and figures of speech may be pressed into the service of explaining action, but that is not one of their essential functions.

Frank (2010a) usefully refers to elemental qualities of narratives as *capacities.* A narrative may be missing any of the three capacities just described. Also, a narrator may merely signal one or more of them without being at all explicit about it (Sandberg 2016). Campaign slogans that allude to stories and thus to moral action and dynamic experience—take Trump's "Make America Great Again" on the campaign trail and beyond—are exemplary. In fact, the latency and indirection of narrative is part of their power. What all this has to do with emotional arousal is the focus of the next chapter.

The three narrative capacities that I have identified may well be capacities of Western narratives, ones that this Western analyst is able to see. In particular, I wonder if Western narratives stress dynamic agency, or at least the dynamic agency of human beings, more than narratives of non-Western people and societies do. Even within our developed society we find radical departures from standard forms, with some of the most marginalized storytellers directing innovation (e.g., Ezzy 2000). Stories, story production, and storytelling are dynamic cultural arenas.

CHAPTER SUMMARY

Enterprises that cause harm on a mass scale make such harm seem reasonable, normal, or desirable. Victims are constructed as deserving or beyond consideration, perpetrators as noble or decent, sometimes because they are not responsible. The move to conceptualize such constructions as discursive follows the linguistic turn in the social sciences. Narratives that sustain mass harm assimilate classifications, metaphors, and other textual features and yet do much more than these because narratives are fundamentally about purposeful, morally relevant conduct in the face of ever-changing circumstances. Narratives connect past and future, such as earlier and later events, selves we were and selves we aspire to become. Narratives also reference other, prior narratives. So narratives situate experiences of agency and structure within lived, time-bound contexts.

Given the close relationship between narrative and human *experience*, it is surprising to find that studies of the enculturation of mass harm mostly focus on legitimation rather than arousal. They concern people's heads, with hearts as an afterthought. They do little to explain the urgency and passion of action. We seem not to have uncovered the essential germ of involvement—its conative aspect, its energy. The nativism that is today gripping Western nations offers new evidence that stories of insiders and outsiders energize even when followers are not necessarily heeding story specifics.

Indeed, emotion has traditionally received scant attention in studies of collective action. Goodwin, Jasper, and Polletta (2001) reflect on the neglect of emotions in social movement research: "The motivation to engage in protest—a process overflowing with emotions—has been largely ignored in recent research because it has so often been taken for granted under the structuralist assumption of objectively given interests" (p. 7; see also Jasper 1998). Yet, even cultural research into social action, such as the important framing perspective, gives emotional mechanisms scant attention (see J. E. Davis 2002; Jasper 1998; Steinberg 1998). The same is true of social research on narratives. Just how they raise the emotional temperature of actors and groups of actors remains unclear.

CHAPTER THREE

Emotion, Narrative, and Transcendence

> She stands over a fish, thinking about certain
> irrevocable mistakes she has made today. Now the
> fish has been cooked, and she is alone with it. The
> fish is for her—there is no one else in the house.
> But she has had a troubling day. How can she eat
> this fish, cooling on a slab of marble? And yet the fish,
> too, motionless as it is, and dismantled from its bones,
> and fleeced of its silver skin, has never been so
> completely alone as it is now: violated in a final
> manner and regarded with a weary eye by this
> woman who has made the latest mistake of her
> day and done this to it.
>
> Lydia Davis (1986, p. 40)

What makes stories moving? How do they move us? And what makes some stories more moving than others? It would be easy to point to stories that highlight supposedly serious issues—those having to do with "life and death"—as the most affecting. Clearly, though, serious issues can be storied in ways that have little emotional impact. Conversely, issues widely viewed as mundane can be recounted in stirring fashion—such as Lydia

Davis's account of a woman preparing her dinner, in this chapter's epigraph. We need to assess both the nature of emotional arousal and the prototypical features of narrative to understand why, in Ed Tan's (1996) words, "to narrate is to produce emotion" (p. 4), and yet that productive capacity is a variable. The last chapter visited those prototypical features; this one dwells on emotion.

The most influential theories of emotion today center on cognition, so I begin my investigation with a broad sweep of these cognitive theories. They posit that emotion depends on appraisals of circumstances that have significance for one's well-being. Cognitive perspectives pave the way for cultural perspectives insofar as we appraise circumstances against cultural models and messages. From cognitive perspectives on emotion and the role of culture therein, I turn to the exceptional capacities of narrative introduced at the end of chapter 2: narrative's integration of meanings, their dynamism, and their explanatory/moralizing functions. I show that each of these capacities is highly relevant to emotion. Next I consider what I call the *figurative pull* of narrative, aesthetic allure that helps to clarify the impact of narrative ambiguity on collective action. The last substantive section of the chapter concerns narrative and spiritual transcendence, or the implications that self-narratives have for being beyond death, whose suggestion generates an emotional charge by alleviating death anxiety (Becker 1973). My ultimate proposal is that narratives have an emotional impact to the extent that they construct our most encompassing desires and identities in a manner that reflects the volatility, sociality, and inscrutability of lived experience.

EMOTION, COGNITION, AND CULTURE: THEORETICAL UNDERSTANDINGS

A long-standing and dominant view, though by no means a unitary one, conceptualizes emotion as fundamentally cognitive in nature—"a certain way of apprehending the world" (Sartre 1948, p. 52). The ancient Greek Stoic philosophy held that emotions stem from judgments and emphasized in particular false judgments that engender emotions such as fear and envy. Emotions more generally and more recently are defined as "valenced reactions to events, agents, or objects, with their particular nature being determined by the way in which the eliciting situation is construed" (Ortony, Clore, and Collins 1988, p. 13). They "arise in response to the meaning structures of given situations; different emotions arise in response to different meaning structures" (Frijda 1988, p. 349).

Ortony, Clore, and Collins (1988) state that "the experience is the sine qua non of emotion" (p. 176).[1] In fact, what we *make* of experience is key. To feel happy, pleased, grief-stricken, angry, or disgusted is to have some idea that we are getting or preserving what we want. To feel angry or disgusted is to have the idea that we have lost or may lose something we want. To feel anxious is to think that we risk losing something of value, including our safety or the safety of significant others. Lazarus (1991) states that cognitive activity with the potential to provoke "consists of a continuing evaluation of the significance of what is happening for one's personal well-being" (p. 144). The distinction between knowledge and appraisal is central to Lazarus's (1991) explanation of why some cognitions affect us emotionally while others do not. Knowledge, for Lazarus, is "our understanding of the way things are and work in general as well as in a specific context" (p. 144). In contrast, appraisal is bound to the personal relevance of what we know. Questions that one asks to assess personal relevance include the following: "Is there harm or threat or am I to be benefited? What kinds of harm or benefit are involved?" (p. 145). Relevance to the agent makes the emotional difference: "Without personal significance, knowledge is cold, or nonemotional. When knowledge touches on one's personal well-being, however, it is hot, or emotional" (p. 144). Thus, while emotion always stems from cognition, cognition does not always produce emotion. The cognition has to matter to us somehow; it has to strike us as making a difference in our lives.

Cognitivists deconstruct emotion in four additional ways that are important for discerning narrative influence. First, emotion is attuned to how we think our *plans* are working out, which brings us, second, to the relevance of *change*. Oatley and Johnson-Laird (1987) write: "The cognitive system adopts an emotion mode at a significant juncture of a plan, i.e., typically . . . when the evaluation (conscious or unconscious) of the likely success of a plan changes" (p. 35). Lazarus (1991) calls emotion "a response to changing or recurrent judgments about oneself in the world" (p. 129). We feel emotional when we "get the news" about something significant to us. Third, emotions are tied to our sense of individual control or *agency*, as Nussbaum (2001) explains: "Emotions. . .involve judgments about important things, judgments in which, appraising an external object as salient for our own well-being, we acknowledge our own neediness and incompleteness before parts of the world that we do not fully control" (p. 19). Nussbaum emphasizes the dramatic charge that perceived powerlessness gives off: "The peculiar depth and the potentially terrifying character of the human emotions derives from the especially complicated thoughts that humans are likely to form about their own need for objects, and about their imperfect control over them" (p. 16). Kemper (1984) offers compatible insights from the sociology of emotions, proposing: "A very large class of human emotions results from real, anticipated, recollected, or imagined outcomes of power and status relations" (p. 371). Power and powerlessness shape societies and the emotions of social actors. Fourth and finally, emotion is closely associated with *identity*. Lazarus (1991) states that "ego-identity is probably involved in all or most emotions" (p. 150). We have feelings about who an event makes us out to be. Nussbaum (2001) underscores emotions' "eudaimonistic" nature: they pertain to "a sense of the self, its goals and projects" (p. 147). For Jasper (1998) the power of identity is primarily affective: "What is difficult to imagine is an identity that is purely cognitive yet strongly held. The 'strength' of an identity comes from its emotional side" (p. 415).

Nussbaum (2001) has achieved an impressive synthesis of many of these ideas in developing her "neo-Stoic" conception of the emotions. She calls emotions "our ways of registering how things are with respect to the external (i.e., uncontrolled) items that we view as salient for our well-being" (p. 4). One of Nussbaum's interventions into the Stoic philosophy is to stress the role of the past in emotional instigation. She writes: "Most of the emotions of adult human beings cannot be well understood without looking at the history of object relations that informs them, as the past shadows the present" (p. 473). "The roots of anger, hatred, and disgust lie very deep in the structure of human life, in our ambivalent relation to our lack of control over objects and the helplessness of our own bodies" (p. 234). Infancy bequeaths amorphous themes of—concerns with—preeminence and powerfulness. Nussbaum thus rejects a view "that tells us to bring every emotion into line with reason's dictates, or the dictates of the person's ideal, whatever that is" (p. 234). Emotions go beyond current evaluation; they also include "a storm of memories and concrete perceptions that swarm around" it (p. 65). Frijda (1988) captures emotions' persistence in his law of conservation of emotional momentum (p. 354): "Certain old pains just do not grow old" (p. 354). What Nussbaum is getting at, though, is not carried-over feeling but carried-over evaluation.

The idea that emotions are based on evaluations of dynamic well-being and selfhood does *not* disqualify individuals who are less developed cognitively from feeling, though their feelings are probably less nuanced. It does not require that we be aware of the evaluations on which our emotions are based (Lazarus 1991; Oatley 1992): it is friendly to the idea that those evaluations have been forgotten or suppressed (Nussbaum 2001). What it does do is emphasize the role that meaning and therefore culture play in our emotional lives, about which Lazarus (1991) advises: "Remember, it is meaning that counts in emotion, not how that meaning is achieved" (p. 160).

Emotions are culturally conditioned in that they are tied to the cultural structures that orient us—namely, standards, goals, and identities. Frijda's (1988) law of comparative feeling speaks to the enculturation of "individual" evaluation against some ideal or standard: "The intensity of emotion depends on the relationship between an event and some frame of reference against which the event is evaluated" (p. 353). For example, I am sad to be terminated from my job insofar as my cultural milieu tells me that having a job is very important for adults. Relatedly, emotions are tied to goals, which always bear a cultural imprint. Frijda's (1988) law of concern states: "Emotions arise in response to events that are important to the individual's goals, motives, or concerns" (p. 351). So, emotions depend on significations of both desire and the circumstances that bear on the fulfillment of desire. One of our goals or desires is to know ourselves and to be known as a certain kind of person. We aspire to be a self that is acceptable if not celebrated. Identity is a steadfast purpose of our plans, and therefore something whose advancement or interference gets us feeling a certain way.

NARRATIVE CAPACITIES AND EMOTION

Thus far we have seen that emotion is shaped by culture. I want to make the further case that emotion is shaped by narrative in particular. If we had to devise an instrument with the capacity to provoke us, we could do no better than to devise narrative. My argument to that effect, you will recall, is organized around the singular work narratives do in (1) integrating meanings, (2) constructing and shutting down the dynamism of agency, and (3) moralizing experience. These capacities are derivative of the regular features of narrative discussed in chapter 1—temporality, causality, action, conflict, transformation, meaning, and situatedness. They were formally introduced in chapter 2. Here I consider the capacities of narratives in light of emotion theories.

Integrating Meanings

Evaluation and meaning are not the exclusive province of narrative (Sternberg 2001). Nonnarrative memoranda, for example, also evaluate. But meaning is a central *concern* of narrative. Narratives are widely seen as trying to establish how things—goals, actions, and events—fit together: they aim for coherence (Brockmeier 2004; Kerby 1991; Linde 1993; Schiffrin 1996; H. White 1987). Or, as Avery Gordon (1997) puts it, "The intricate web of connections that characterizes any event or problem *is the story*" (p. 20; emphasis in original). When connections are forged between aspects and experiences of the self—in stories of self—the result is a (provisionally) coherent self, or identity. Moreover, narratives integrate meanings. They forge a unified common sense, albeit one that is always provisional and subject to misunderstanding and reinterpretation, rather than the piecemeal points that are presented in a nonnarrative memo. Narrative's pursuit and integration of meaning represent a baseline condition for its other capacities.

Constructing and Shutting Down Dynamic Agency

The meanings that capture our attention in stories are those that concern our capacity or the capacity of protagonists to achieve our or their goals. Narrative drama rides mainly on the waves of the protagonist's level of control over such achievement. Because autonomy is a basic drive—a state of being that humans universally aspire to—it is not surprising that it is greatly implicated in our emotional lives. Nussbaum (2001) states that "emotions are appraisals or value judgments, which ascribe to things and persons outside the person's own control great importance for that person's own flourishing" (p. 4). We get emotional about agency. Katz (1999, p. 148) thus conceives of emotions as "dialectical tensions between doing and being done by interaction with others."

In stories as in life, circumstances are unstable. Things change, and stories recount that change. For philosopher Louis Mink (1970): "Surprises and contingencies are the stuff of stories" (p. 545). Literary scholar Peter Brooks (1984) insists on the dynamism of plot and therefore narrative—the fact that it moves events toward some purpose. Indeed, it is difficult to speak of plot without using physical and especially directional metaphors. Plot *moves* the story toward some point. It gives the *direction* that the protagonist is going in. Story *line* and *arc* are frequently used in reference to plot. More lyrically, Brooks calls plot "a kind of arabesque or squiggle toward the end" (p. 104). Plot drives the audience of a narrative toward the imagined closure of storied events.

Precariousness is central to stories and to their emotional power. Sternberg (2001) describes three "narrative master forces"—suspense, curiosity, and surprise (p. 117), each of which reflects instability. Mar and Oatley (2008) emphasize "the inclusion of dramatic climaxes" as constituting narrative impact (p. 178). The volatility of plot heightens our attention: it promotes absorption (Bezdek et al. 2015). Thus, narratives that compel us capture something true about the continuous but unpredictable rhythms of our lives. As for feeling, emotion theorist Frijda (1988) presents, among others, the law of change: "Emotions are elicited not so much by the presence of favorable or unfavorable conditions, but by actual or expected changes in favorable or unfavorable conditions" (p. 353). Besides: "The greater the change, the stronger the subsequent emotion" (p. 353). In addition, we are most affected by a favorable outcome when our well-being was or is in doubt. We are more joyful when our beloved cat returns home after being lost for days than when she returns home at 5:00 p.m. as she always does. Frijda's law of affective contrast (p. 353) explains this phenomenon. Narrative suspense and thus interest are sustained when the outcomes that are important for well-being and survival are not assured. We are waiting to see what will happen, in our own lives as in the lives of other protagonists.

Beyond interest, I propose that we feel *gratified* by stories that *shut down* dynamic agency—that freeze volatility. The fact that stories are dynamic means that both the happy and the dismal circumstance may turn. Depending on when "the end" is called, it is favorable or unfavorable. Closure, or declaring the story over, provides a sense of satisfaction rather than excitement.[2]

Moralizing Experience

Stories do not merely describe change. They explain it, setting out causal relationships. Explanations are a key site of morality because explanations responsibilize experience. They assign (or vacate) blame or credit. Nussbaum (2001) calls emotions "value-laden ways of understanding the world" (p. 88), and the very same can be said of narratives. Frank (2010b) observes: "Stories teach which actions are good and which are bad; without stories there would be no sense of action as ethical" (p. 665).

Stories convey moral lessons through their characters, relating what characters experience as a result of their ethically significant actions. We judge story characters according to obviously moral criteria, as, for example, good, innocent, or heroic versus bad, threatening, or tainted. Narratives draw symbolic boundaries (Lamont and Molnár 2002) between characters, and they distinguish between the protagonist before and after harm-relevant events. Thus, for example, Feldman (1991) points out a distinction drawn within Irish Republican Army narratives between the hardman and the gunman, characters that align with and explain past and present violence. Narratives also bridge or blur existing boundaries, as Lydia Davis bridges a boundary between species in her short story "The Fish" (see the epigraph to this chapter) and as violence recruiters (to war or terrorism, for example) blur differences between would-be fighters in calling for united action. But narratives are better known for drawing distinctions than erasing them. The most inflammatory narratives tend to characterize their principals in diametrically opposed ways. Stark oppositions are a mainstay of *Dabiq*, a magazine published by the jihadist militant organization known as the Islamic State, as in the foreword to its penultimate issue: "For nearly two years, Muslims in the lands of the Khilāfah have watched their beloved brothers, sisters, and children being relentlessly bombed by crusader warplanes. The scenes of carnage, of blood and limbs scattered in the streets, have become commonplace for the believers. The yearning for revenge has taken seed and has grown steadily in the hearts of the grieving widows, distressed orphans, and solemn soldiers; and the fruits are ready for harvest" (*Dabiq* 2016, p. 4). On the side of good are beloved family members and solemn soldiers. The enemy here is in the form of "crusader warplanes," so while "the believers" are all innocence, the enemy is all aggression, objectified as weapons.

The distance between the characters, the achievement of "ideological squaring" (van Dijk 1993), confers drama. Whereas we generally root for the virtuous, we may also identify with those morally complex individuals who do bad things *and* demonstrate certain admired virtues (Sanders and Tsay-Vogel 2016). Sanders and Tsay-Vogel (2016) note: "More positive moral judgements ... do not always lead to affinity" (p. 236). In their study of moral reactions to Harry Potter books and films, they found that audience members admired and consequently identified with the morally complex and even tainted story characters—so-called antiheroes. Likewise, we make varied meanings of our own moral complexity. The contradictory elements we find in ourselves may even stir us, as I discuss shortly in regard to narrative ambiguity. In addition to arousing, characterization can also *dampen* feeling. When we construct others as foreign or minimally drawn, we are likely to feel apathy regarding their well-being. The key to all these construals, ultimately, is our well-being—whether the Other does or can undermine it.

The project of *self*-narrative has received much attention in the social sciences during the last several decades. Self-narratives construct what protagonist-narrators have going on, what they are like, and especially their position and power relative to others in the narrative universe (see Presser 2013, p. 19). As Somers (1994) puts it: "It is through narrativity that we come to know, understand, and make sense of the social world, and it is through narratives and narrativity that we constitute our social identities" (p. 606). Whereas figurative expressions may ("I was in a dark mood") or may not ("a dark day") communicate about the self, narratives specialize in it. Of course, not all narratives patently concern the self, which is to say, not all narratives are self-narratives. However, we are most engaged by narratives that explicitly or implicitly concern who we are or who someone like us is. Schank and Berman (2002) observe: "Listeners will relate most to the parts of the story that speak to their personal experience" (p. 304). Note, though, that we find in a wide array of stories some relevance to the self.

THE FIGURATIVE PULL

Not just stories grab us: art in general has that effect (Torossian 1937). Among the most affecting dimensions of art is figuration, such as is achieved through metaphor.

Figurative expression generally refers to particular devices, including metaphor, simile, metonymy, litote, synecdoche, personification, metalepsis, oxymoron, sarcasm, irony, idiom, rhetorical questions, and more. Metaphors deploy a concept from one domain to signify another: for instance, "I was feeling down," where a concept from the orientational domain ("down") is used to signify an emotion (sadness). Metonymy is referencing one thing by another thing with which it is associated, including a salient feature, such as a "hand" in place of help. Litote is a form of understatement where a negative construction denotes a positive one: "not bad" instead of "good," for example. Sarcasm involves saying something starkly different and even opposite to what one truly means, as in "Well *that* was a great party!" In each of these illustrations the communicator takes a circuitous route to articulating meaning.

Gibbs, Leggitt, and Turner (2002) concluded from their own and others' experimental research that "metaphorical language both reflects and induces greater emotional intensity than literal language" (p. 139). The finding that figurative or nonliteral language is distinctly moving is also borne out by psychophysiological research. Rojo, Ramos, and Valenzuela (2014) observed that participants' heart rates were reduced when English-to-Spanish translations of stories replaced figurative expressions with literal ones: literal language was less exciting. Citron and colleagues (2016) found that emotional engagement, as measured by activation of the amygdala in the brain, increased with the number of metaphors in a story to which participants were exposed, controlling for the story's complexity. On the production side, Fainsilber and Ortony (1987) determined that speakers used more metaphors when they described their *feelings* about a past experience than when they described their *behaviors* related to the experience. They also found that the more emotionally intense that experience, the more often the speakers used metaphors.

Like every other discursive form (see Lakoff and Johnson 1980), narratives are replete with figures of speech. "Ask people about some aspect of their lives, and metaphor will inevitably burst forth, sometimes dominating the narrative" (Gibbs 1994, p. 120). However, narratives are not only populated with figures of speech. Narratives are *themselves* figurative. They are symbolic constructions of lives, persons, groups, nations, and epochs. By design they say something beyond the particular episodes they recount. Narratives stand in for flows of experience. What is the nature of the figurative pull—of narrative in particular? I contend that it resides in gaps, which demand that active conceptual connections be drawn, and which stimulate ingress of the stuff of memory.

Gaps and Connections

Figurative speech or text requires audiences to fill in gaps for the sake of understanding. Filling in such gaps in turn requires conceptual connections that are not given but knowable from elsewhere in the arsenal of human experience. The author of figurative speech or text assumes that the audience can forge those connections. When Lydia Davis (1986) writes in her novel, "And yet the fish, too, motionless as it is, and dismantled from its bones, and fleeced of its silver skin, has never been so completely alone as it is now," she is saying that the human protagonist has never been so completely alone as she is now, signaled by the word "too." Davis is counting on readers relating the human protagonist's troubles, mistakes, and physical solitude on this evening to a more existential condition, a kind of solitude that is like death in its gloom and its lastingness. The author constructs the reader as not just a knower but a member of a community of knowers. Figuration builds relationships among the parties to an exchange (e.g., between author and audience) as it builds relationships among experiences.

A similar phenomenon pertains to self-narratives. The self-narrative contains gaps that reflect the open-endedness of meaning and thus experience. The self-narrator convenes a dialogue among various perspectives—those of others and her own, now and before—as she connects different experiences. For example, in April 2016 Rodrigo Duterte, then campaigning for the presidency of the Philippines, storied his response to the gang rape and murder of an imprisoned missionary during his extended term as mayor of Davao City (Andrews 2016): "I was angry because she was raped. That's one thing. But she was so beautiful. The mayor should have been first." This joke/story plays on the audacious incongruity between being angry about a rape, presumably on moral grounds, and being disappointed not to have raped. In addition, Duterte is making fun of the cultural expectation that a politician (or anyone else) condemn violence—without saying anything explicit about such an expectation. He revels in transgressions such as these and connects to others who would similarly find the transgressions a source of fun: he thus achieves solidarity—indeed, a dangerous masculine tribalism—even while he breaks free of presumably shared social norms. The seductive energy of his story is tied up with exploring how socially encumbered or free he is (see Katz 1988). The figurative pull is the process wherein language allows us to dream a different state of (in)dependence than we think we inhabit. The example of Duterte's short story may be unusual, not least because it is strongly motivated politically and rhetorically, and yet this example illustrates something we all do with our stories—associate and disassociate ways of seeing the world and thereby attach to and detach from other "seers."

Memory Traces

The compulsion of figurative discourse, including all narratives, has an additional, seemingly intra-individual aspect to be considered. Ortony (1975) proposes that metaphors are affecting because they bring out the lushness of the original domain of experience: they "avoid discretizing the perceived continuity of experience and are thus closer to experience and consequently more vivid and memorable" (p. 53). The proximity of narrative to lived experience was previously discussed in terms of the dynamism that they share. The present point is that we sense the past lurking in the present as uniquely authentic and thus compelling. But something more: we are emotionally tethered to our own early experiences. Recall the connections Nussbaum (2001) draws between emotion and object relations, discussed earlier in this chapter. Nussbaum observes that "the cognitive content of emotions arrives embedded in a complex narrative history" (p. 179). Along similar lines, Hogan (2003) proposes that "our affective response to a situation, real or fictional, is not a response to an isolated moment, but to the entire sequence of events in which that moment is located, whether explicitly or implicitly" (p. 5). Hogan's overarching thesis is that paradigmatic stories, including the stories we ourselves author and tell, explicate (culturally familiar) sequences of happening and feeling. Whence the provocation of those stories?

Seeking to understand emotional responses to literature, Hogan (2003) develops a "cognitive theory of poetic feeling" (p. 45), which crosses Sanskrit theory of aesthetics dating from the second century b.c.e., particularly *dhvani*, or suggestiveness, with current cognitive science. That integration is fruitful for thinking about real-world narrative impacts as well, as I will show.

Rasa is the emotion we feel concerning a work of art. Dhvani is the suggested or unstated meaning of the work—literally (in Sanskrit) its "tone" or its resonance (Edgerton 1936). Ānandavardhana described certain works as achieving *rasadhvani*—the dhvani of rasa. Whereas rasas are "evoked in a reader by words, sentences, topics, and so on"—literal content—rasadhvani is conjured from "the clouds of nondenumerable, nonsubstitutable, nonpropositional suggestions that surround these texts" (Hogan 2003, p. 51). Subsequently, Abhinavagupta proposed a psychological mechanism for rasadhvani: "Through dhvani, the literary work activates memory traces in the mind of the reader ... without bringing these memories into consciousness" (p. 52). Memories rush in where texts leave things unsaid. At the same time, the concept of *dhvani* directs us to the active engagement of audiences in their own captivation.

Theories of reading point to active engagement as well. Iser (1972, 1978) is well known for insisting that the reader who gets swept away by a work of fiction is a coproducer of the meaning of the text. Gerrig (1993) reiterates the position: readers "must use their own experiences of the world to bridge gaps in texts" (p. 17). Boruah (1988) emphasizes the role of both imagination and evaluation in producing emotional responses to fictional stories. Imagination plays a role in our emotional responses to nonfiction stories as well: "The narrative presented to the reader is transformed into something worthwhile and interesting by assimilating it to culturally encoded norms of what is natural, acceptable, and interesting" (L. Herman and Vervaeck 2009, p. 120). This view accords with theories of aesthetic experience generally, which recognize the arousal potential of art as dependent on an active audience (see, e.g., Matravers 1991). It is also supported by the finding that metaphor production taps into the retrieval of memories (Benedek et al. 2014). The idea that affect pulls from memory is also channeled in Lazarus's (1991) theory of emotion as adaptation: "Much in life is a restatement of past struggles, which as a feature of our personal history is an integral part of the emotion process.... In effect, many appraisal decisions have already been all but made, and need only the appropriate environmental cue to trigger them. Deliberation is not needed to appraise these instances, because the appraisal patterns have, as it were, already been set in advance" (p. 151). Frank (2010a) observes that some stories resonate because they are congruent with an internalized set of stories (see also Fleetwood 2016). He adapts Bourdieu's concept of habitus to describe a "*repertoire* of stories that a person at least recognizes and that a group shares": "Narrative habitus describes the embodied sense of attraction, indifference, or propulsion people feel in response to stories; the intuitive, usually tacit sense that some story is *for us* or not for us; that it expresses possibilities of which we are or can be part, or that it represents a world in which we have no stake" (Frank 2010a, p. 53; emphasis in original). The position these scholars hold in common is that certain stories move us because they call to mind past experience. We have been down the road they recall before.

Here, sociology inserts that labeling, experience, and memory all have a cultural basis (Howard 1995), extending Durkheim's insistence that collective representations are not reducible to individual minds. Zerubavel's (1997) sociology of memory emphasizes the fact that we share some of "our" memories in common with others, but only certain others; that norms govern what we must remember and what we can or should forget; that our recall is most successful when the information corresponds with conventional expectations; that we "remember" much more than we have experienced as individuals; and that social repositories of memories, such as stories and poetry, help us retain them. Our society helps determine our memories. This cultural contribution is active and present, and it is political, as battles over Confederate monuments in the United States clearly show.[3] Sociology of memory summons a critical appraisal of memory-making, including the banishment of certain experiences on the basis that they did not occur or do not much matter. Partly fashioned from the residues of a barely remembered or negated past, the force of culture can be uncanny (Gordon 1997; Sharpe 2016).

Ambiguity

Researchers theorizing the role of narrative in social action have discussed the quality of figurativeness less than they have *ambiguity*, which is another kind of indirectness. Figurativeness involves representing one thing as something else—something evidently different, including something more basic or more encompassing, than a thing "actually" is. Ambiguity may be achieved via figuration but it is just as likely to consist in discursive gaps and equivocations.[4] Sociological studies of ambiguity give clues to the figurative pull in action.

The more ambiguous a story, the more people can make that story their own. Thus, Halverson, Goodall, and Corman (2011, p. 187) observe that leaving out the identity of the people's rescuer, as is the case in certain Islamist extremist narratives, constructs an invitational edge. Among violence stories shared by drug dealers, Sandberg, Tutenges, and Copes (2015) similarly find: "The ambiguity of stories makes it possible for narrators to explore existential issues without having a clear answer and to continuously adjust evaluations and content" (p. 1171), including evaluations and content from interlocutors. Polletta (2006, pp. 172–74) identifies three sources of ambiguity in social movement narratives: (1) polysemy, or the multiple meanings of words used; (2) perspectival, or opacity as to the source of the story's point of view; and (3) semantic dissonance or combining story elements in unusual ways. She argues that ambiguity is "politically effective" (p. 174), for example: "Ambiguity as polysemy made it possible for people and groups to forge agreement across diverse interests" (p. 174). Relatedly, narrators convey hegemonic ideas in presuppositions or silences, which effectively shelter those ideas from critique.

We have seen that it is in the nature of stories to tread lightly around perspective. Some of the most compelling stories offer only "partial cues" as to what happened and what the story means (Auyoung 2013). In actual social exchanges, narratives are very often told in fragments or through reference to narratives not actually told. We regularly exchange parcels of stories, which scholars refer to as tropes (Sandberg 2016), abbreviated stories (Schank and Abelson 1995, p. 3), small stories (Bamberg and Georgakopoulou 2008), and fragments (Halverson, Goodall, and Corman 2011, p. 22). These can be brief plot summaries or even single terms that are closely associated with a presumably well-known story: think "superpredator" or "9/11." The mere mention of these terms can elicit immediate recognition and create some provisional consensus. Narrative cues offer a way for storytellers to conjure, efficiently and noncontroversially, the dominant understandings and original emotions associated with the benchmark narrative, while also gesturing about the narrator as a cultural insider. Story brevity does not preclude resonance, and sometimes actually enhances it because it allows us to forge taken-for-granted and/or personal associations.

Researchers have tended to view ambiguity as subterfuge, or a way of bypassing recipients' critical thinking. I am not opposed to that view and see considerable evidence for it, but I also take note of the impossibility of uniform meaning and clarity in narrative. I submit that the enigmatic story may bear an essential message about who we are and what our lives are like.

Narrative operates *through* suggestiveness and thus, as discussed earlier, through conceptual and social connections. The pull of suggestiveness has gone largely unnoticed in sociological studies. Suggestiveness in ordinary English has an erotic connotation, as does seduction. That students of the literary arts use these terms to describe narrative impacts suggests that narrative be considered as extending an invitation to *relate.* As Chambers (1984) states: "There is a form of seduction that consists of holding the 'seducee' at arm's length. Narrative seduction, then, seems as complex and varied in its tactics as are the erotic seductions of everyday life; and its range, from active enterprise, through the 'simple' invitation, to a carefully calculated 'refusal,' is not dissimilar to what can be observed wherever people relate sexually to one another" (p. 217). The range of seduction strategies to which Chambers refers corresponds to expressions of narrative ambiguity in social life. Without necessarily pursuing a psychosexual explanation of narrative seduction, we may register the felt truth of the metaphor.

SPIRITUAL TRANSCENDENCE

Again, the narratives we tell account for an action or series of actions, but their message is always bigger. "What happened" is interesting as the sort of thing that happens or *can* happen (Aristotle 1996). In particular, shaping lives around stories gives those lives not just meaning but spiritual meaning. Life stories allow us to outlive time and/in our bodies. Such stories become sacred entities as they leave behind "the given and bland reality of the everyday animal world" (Becker 1973, p. 240). The desire for transcendent meaning is in my view most lucidly described by anthropologist Ernest Becker (1973): "The distinctive human problem from time immemorial has been the need to spiritualize human life, to lift it onto a special immoral plane, beyond the cycles of life and death that characterize all other organisms" (p. 231). Without such meaning we fall into despair and neurosis, which Becker considered as "a widespread problem because of the disappearance of convincing dramas of heroic apotheosis of man" (p. 190). Becker's ideas help to illuminate the close relationship between life stories and sublimity.

We are all short of time, whereas story characters live for eternity. Narratives construct a self that promises to endure after death. Becker argues that human beings' fear of death is universal and far-reaching. Unlike other animals, humans are aware of their own mortality. That awareness causes dread, the antidotes to which are establishing one's special value in the world and/or repressing the truth of one's existence. First, we try to achieve "heroism," which Becker conceives as our "ultimate usefulness to creation": "The hope and belief is that the things that man creates in society are of lasting worth and meaning, that they outlive or outshine death and decay, that man and his products count" (p. 5). Since "to see the world as it really is is devastating and terrifying" (p. 60), we also repress our fate. For Becker the fear of powerlessness is consubstantial with fear of mortality because death is "the final sucking up, the total submergence and negation" (p. 54). Our defenses, then, allow us "to feel a basic sense of self-worth, of meaningfulness, of power" (p. 55). We must erect them: Becker refers to "a *necessary* and basic dishonesty about oneself and one's whole situation (p. 55; emphasis in original). Against Freud, who theorized repression in terms of drives, specifically sexual ones, Becker contends that repression is induced by fear of death and the ineffectualness associated with it.

Becker's ideas inform terror management theory, which posits that humans' cultural creations, including their worldviews, are strategies for creating enduring meaning and thus easing terror in the face of mortality (see Van Marle and Maruna 2010). But we are not merely relieved by cultural creation: we are exalted, as Becker (1973) notes: "The urge to immortality is not a simple reflex of the death-anxiety but a reaching out by one's whole being toward life" (pp. 152–53). We yearn "to become part of such a larger and higher wholeness as religion has always represented" (p. 199). Thus, death anxiety has the potential to energize rather than sedate us. Indeed, defiance of the circumstance of powerlessness can, Becker suggests, lead us to perpetrate great harm: "Carried to its demonic extreme this defiance gave us Hitler and Vietnam: a rage against our impotence, a defiance of our animal condition, our pathetic creature limitations. If we don't have the omnipotence of gods, we at least can destroy like Gods" (p. 85).

What Becker mostly leaves out of that formulation of harm-causing defiance is its essential cultural framing. Yet, he had earlier insisted on the symbolic nature of human existence: "Man has a symbolic identity that brings him sharply out of nature. He is a symbolic self, a creature with a name, a life history. He is a creator with a mind that soars out to speculate about atoms and infinity, who can place himself imaginatively at a point in space and contemplate bemusedly his own planet. This immense expansion, this dexterity, this ethereality, this self-consciousness gives to man literally the status of a small god in nature, as the Renaissance thinkers knew" (p. 26). Becker assures us of the enculturation of our efforts at denial and heroism, the fact that "almost everyone consents to earn his immortality in the popular ways mapped out by societies everywhere, in the beyond of others and not their own" (p. 170). The stories we live out, for the sake of living forever, are those certified by the cultural milieu we inhabit.

Becker's (1973) ideas about the essential human dilemma of mortal insignificance and its consequences help explain the narratives we create and the pull they exert: "Man cannot endure his own littleness unless he can translate it into meaningfulness on the largest possible level" (p. 196). Yet, not only grand myths achieve meaningfulness and beat back mortality (Nell 2002). Characters of our considerably less epic stories live for eternity insofar as some meaning is ascribed to our having lived at all.

CHAPTER SUMMARY

Narrative is a highly affecting cultural form. Cognitive theories of emotion postulate that emotions stem from our evaluations of how we are doing vis-à-vis our goals. Narratives are unparalleled vehicles for constructing our standing in the world, insofar as they consolidate the essential meaning of important experiences, reflect our shifting and comparative agency, and project ethical, transcendent significance. The more attuned a narrative is to the dynamic, moral aspect of human experience, the more arousing it tends to be. The inherent figurativeness and ambiguity of stories and storytelling invite active engagement in order to build moral meaning.

Some narratives are more affecting than others. We are provoked by trajectories whose uncertain outcomes are consequential to who we are and which reach for unending significance. Such narratives connect to a barely recalled or even suppressed past with its primitive but commanding concerns of existential significance and power, and they counteract our universal dread of death and insignificance.

The next two chapters highlight the different kinds of emotional response induced by stories. At one extreme are stories that cultivate rage or exhilaration and a sense of urgency. At the other extreme are stories that generate a mood of agreeability or satisfaction.

CHAPTER FOUR

The Invitational Edge of Underdog Stories

The kind of harm that is usually called violence—corporeal, direct, and intentional—is not the only kind there is. It is neither the most prevalent nor the most damaging. Nonetheless, it gets the most public attention and is the most recognizably immoral. Stories that promote violence typically generate palpable excitement. The purpose of this chapter is to discern the nature of that emotional charge—in other words, to grasp the drama of dramatic stories. Among dramatic stories my specific focus is the underdog story, whose basic point is that the righteous, though few and meek, can triumph over the unjust, who are great and mighty. Action films and video games are replete with stories of the aggrieved and often misunderstood hero going it alone (sometimes with a sidekick or tiny contingent) against powerful enemies. A secular version is told by police who conjure themselves as soldiers occupying dangerous war zones where civilians cannot be trusted (Kurtz and Upton 2017). The major religions offer several underdog stories. In the Islamic tradition they include those of the Battle of Karbala and the

Battle of Badr (Halverson, Goodall, and Corman 2011). The classic biblical underdog story of David and Goliath is told by adherents of all three of the Abrahamic religions—Islam, Christianity, and Judaism.

Using several different renderings of the underdog story but especially those associated with terrorism, I argue that the story arouses us because it put us in mind of a deep sense of wrongful vulnerability in the world only to assuage that sense through triumphant, transcendent action. The story tells us that we are both more powerful and less alone than we imagined ourselves to be—less alone, but also special. The story draws on extreme distinctions between beings in the world and between our own actual and potential, rightful capacities. In general, the dramatic story sets into sharp relief states of being, identities, and capacities that we covet but are always tenuous, if achievable at all.

Many if not most theories that explain violence in terms of subordination or grievance, which in criminology include both critical and mainstream perspectives, overlook the fact that actors are actively involved in projects of enculturated narrative identities that are often at the same time personally relished. Actors' sorry circumstances may seem and feel desperate, their reactions unfortunate. Yet, those reactions may at the same time resound with a sense of cultural rightness and pulsate with excitement (Ferrell et al. 2004). The boy who is challenged to do masculinity violently, who lacks other ways of doing it according to structured action theory (Messerschmidt 2000), is playing out a plot that the actor and others may bemoan but nonetheless find meaningful and thrilling. The predicted action sequences are storied. And the stories do not simply tell us how to behave; they cause us to feel something.

CRISIS AND ACTION

All stories, including the most basic and mundane, recount shifts in circumstances. What I am calling *dramatic stories* feature radical shifts, such as from tranquillity to turmoil. More specifically, some crisis arises. By crisis I mean a potentially devastating event that comes on suddenly. Dramatic stories posit (re)action as urgent, necessary, and even inevitable. Action always has strong *moral* implications within the story even when it is warranted on practical grounds, such as to oppose policy that would be detrimental to the environment.

What I am calling *underdog stories* emphasize the fact that action is honorable, even morally ordained, but the success of action seems doubtful. Underdog stories convey both of these messages through character. They star a particular hero or heroic group whose trajectory from impotence or victimhood to triumph is stark. The virtuous protagonist in the underdog story takes morally weighty action against the odds. Underdog stories are thus perfectly suited to insurgencies and protest movements of all kinds, where adversaries have more resources—weapons, legal power, personnel, and so forth—than protagonists do. By definition, insurgencies and protest movements contest the status quo but currently lack political standing. In all underdog stories the fight is against some undue hardship or unjust circumstance including a morally offensive threat. Underdog stories may be said to deploy what Gamson (1992) calls an injustice frame. The injustice, like every other element of the story, can be assembled creatively, though within the parameters of cultural understandings. A cancer diagnosis received by a good person can be related through an underdog story, so long as having and resisting cancer are characterized in morally exalted terms, as they are in the West. President Donald Trump conceived of regulations as leaving the U.S. banking industry "devastated and unable to properly serve the public," in the face of strong evidence to the contrary (Goldstein and Cowley 2017). The financial firms are victims who furthermore cannot help others, which is what underdog heroes do.

The crisis in the underdog story may not yet have taken place: it may be depicted as impending. Domestic terrorist Anders Behring Breivik lamented a coming crisis from immigration of Muslims to Norway: "It would now only take 50–70 years before we, the Europeans, are in a minority" (quoted in Sandberg 2013, p. 72). The crisis claim may be altogether dubious given current structural arrangements. Lai (2015, who studied organized political opposition to strategies of prevention and intervention into anti-LGBT bullying in the United States, remarks: "The future is bleak in the event of anti-bullying legislation passing. For example, [politician Michele] Bachmann asked: 'Will it get to the point where we are completely stifling free speech and expression?'" (pp. 73–74). Protagonists may themselves manufacture the crisis, as Jackson-Jacobs (2004) shows in his research on young men starting street fights they are sure to lose. Narrators have nearly free rein with the events, real or fictional, that they identify as threatening—the "moral panics" they construct (S. Cohen 2011).

The crisis may not be well and truly over by the end of the story, in which case the protagonist vows never to stop fighting or signals such a commitment, garnering admiration. Underdog stories are about the qualities that heroes demonstrate and not their tangible achievements.

STARK DIFFERENCES

For the sake of motivating action, it is not enough that the dramatic story—underdog or any other—depict a crisis, as Philip Smith's (2005) comparative analysis of political standoffs between nations shows. Crises can be narrated in rather different ways, with different ramifications for action (e.g., state policy). The drama that inheres in dramatic stories is due in large part to the drawing of stark differences or boundaries (Lamont and Molnár 2002). In underdog stories, the boundaries are both material (small/weak versus big/strong) and moral (good versus bad). Correspondingly, they pertain to both process and character. Stark material and moral differences highlight the badness of the opponent, the near impossibility of defeating him (or it), and the virtue of the hero.

Material Contrasts

A distinctive feature of the underdog story as compared with other dramatic stories is that protagonist and foe differ markedly in their cache of tangible resources. The underdog is weaker and/or outnumbered. Objectively outnumbered elites (e.g., colonists, police officers) cast themselves as underdogs despite their measurable and otherwise touted social and political dominance—indeed, despite other sorts of material control such as weaponry and position. The most seemingly powerful actors summon underdog stories: witness contemporary right-wing movements in which white men are allegedly put upon by ethnic minorities feminists, LGBTQ people, and others. Speculation about being outnumbered in the future fulfills the material contrast criterion of the underdog story as well. As we have seen elsewhere, tellers can be quite resourceful and selective in representing such.

Underdog stories encourage those who fight but suffer to persist. Those who would bolster mass participation in arduous struggles against powerful enemies use them in just this way. A call to jihad from Abdallah Azzam, a key leader of the Al Qaeda terrorist organization who is considered to have masterminded its strategy of violent global attacks, points to asymmetries of strength in his 1987 book *Join the Caravan*: "The Prophet's companions were only a handful of men, compared to the troops that overturned Chosroes' throne and tarnished Caesar's glory" (Kepel and Milelli 2008, p. 118). Halverson, Goodall, and Corman (2011) observe that the Battle of Badr narrative "tells the story of a pivotal turn in the course of Islamic history and it serves as a powerful lesson for all Muslims to be firm in their faith through trials and adversity, even in the face of seemingly impossible odds or certain death" (p. 53), noting that "Badr has remained a normative reference point for al-Qaeda's vision of its military operations up to the present" (p. 55). Similarly, the Battle of Karbala master narrative emboldens: "The existence of a superior military force, which may otherwise discourage rebellion or dissent, carries little power in the face of a master narrative where the hero to be emulated accepts martyrdom in his role as God's chosen leader in earth" (p. 93).

From these examples one might suppose that underdog appeals are devised to reassure insurgents of success and thus to allay any fears they may have. The story tells us that we ought not hesitate to act—we ought not doubt the moment or our abilities: all will be well. That may be so, but I would also argue that the long odds are a crucial aspect of the draw. What invites exertion is not the ease of winning but the honor of the trial.

Studying terrorist discourse, Cordes (2001) determines that "there is nobility and honor in the courage and determination of an oppressed party who dares to strike out at the 'oppressor'" (p. 60). The underdog's goal of realizing a drastic reversal indicates great courage. These stories give heart, but they also seduce through preferred moral positions.

Moral Contrasts

The material resources of the adversary are outweighed by the moral resources of the hero, as David reflects to Goliath, "the Philistine" he attacked and killed: "David said to the Philistine, 'You come against me with sword and spear and javelin, but I come against you in the name of the Lord of hosts, the God of the armies of Israel, whom you have defied'" (1 Samuel 17:45). The underdog story highlights the superiority of divine or moral capacities over the earthly kind. God, or good, empowers. As such, the heroic underdog's triumph gains in moral significance with the immensity of the obstacles he encounters along the way.

The adversary is reduced to evil, whereas the protagonist (who is also reduced) is all good. They are moral opposites. Loseke (2003) astutely observes that "while victims are characters who do no harm, villains are characters who only do harm" (p. 90). The Shiite master narrative of the Battle of Karbala depicts this kind of schism: "Husayn and his companions, especially 'Abbas, are the archetypal heroes and martyrs of the narrative. They are portrayed as brave, noble, and willing to sacrifice everything in the struggle against injustice and oppression. On the opposing side is the cruel, treacherous, and barbaric army of the antagonist, the archetypal tyrant Yazid, the Umayyad Caliph" (Halverson, Goodall, and Corman 2011, p. 87).

The apocalyptic narrative central to violent antiabortion activism in Mason's (2002) study similarly identifies "some particular people as pro-life warriors and others as conspiratorial enemies of life" (p. 191). Smith states that the apocalyptic narrative that generates calls to war "involves the most intense character polarization that involves the highest and lowest of human motivations" (p. 26). Frank (2010a) states: "Stories are entirely too effective at demonizing" (p. 76). My point is that they demonize as they thematize the pursuit of goodness. Hence we see degraded persons investing in self-stories that elevate them above more horrible others. A case in point is Ugelvik's (2015) research finding that stories told by prisoners in Norway drew a sharp distinction between themselves—proper criminals—and rapists. Such stories do ethical work on the self, "aimed at resolving one of the fundamental problems of the prison experience: namely that of being positioned as an immoral other by the society outside" (Ugelvik 2015, p. 37). With polarization, it appears, comes emotion. Jasper observes (1998): "Demonization fuels powerful emotions for social movements" (p. 412). Ronald Jacobs (2002) makes the same point: "By arranging the characters of a narrative in binary relations to one another, and doing the same thing with the descriptive terms attached to those characters, narratives help to charge social life with evaluative and dramatic intensity" (p. 216). What accounts for that intensity?

THE ALLURE OF NEGATIVITY

First, the intensity of feeling from the story matches the intensity of the moral mission, which matches the intensity of evil. Emotions run high because the struggle matters so terribly much. That good conceptually depends on evil is axiomatic for structural anthropologists beginning with Claude Lévi-Strauss, who consider binary oppositions as parcel to universal worldviews. Well-being is constructed out of devastation.

So, for example, Halverson, Goodall, and Corman (2011) deduce what the major narratives associated with Islamist extremism have in common: "Together, the master narratives, their story forms, and archetypes, constitute a rhetorical vision of a dangerous world for Islam" (p. 190), while Maan (2015) observes: "The Master narrative in most terrorist calls to violence is titled 'Victim'" (p. 18). Adverse conditions, dark prospects, and tragic events are the central motifs of the most dramatic stories, notwithstanding whatever happy outcomes they might precede. Agency is dedicated to opposing the former as much as it is to attaining the latter.

Second, studies in psychology point to a more grounded dimension of negativity's allure. Consistently, negative feelings are found to exert a stronger grip than do positive feelings. Negative events get our attention more than positive ones do (N.K. Smith et al. 2003). An expansive review of research leads Baumeister et al. (2001) to conclude that "events involving bad emotions remain more salient on people's minds than events involving good emotions" (p. 333). In addition: "Bad emotions generally produce more cognitive processing and have other effects on behavior that are stronger than positive emotions" (p. 334). Jasper (1998) observes these tendencies at play in social movements: "Abstract norms of justice gain some power from the positive emotions associated with them—hope, joy, compassion—but probably not enough to motivate action in the absence of a contrast with an unjust situation and the negative emotions—a sense of threat, outrage, anger, fear—associated with it" (p. 414). Sociologists have rarely confronted the ramifications of people's attraction to negativity, though cultural criminologists come close to the issue via the appeal of transgression, which is one aspect of the general phenomenon. The self-help literature offers explanations for the draw of badness based on psychic and spiritual dysfunction. Popular spiritual writer Eckhart Tolle (2006), for example, describes a person's "pain-body" as the internal repository of emotional pain from the past. Such writings relate the phenomenological past to present evaluation. They acknowledge that (others') negativity can motivate us, and not only because it shines a light on (our) goodness.

In the underdog story, all negativity belongs to the enemy. The heroic underdog is altogether virtuous, though some in his camp are faulted for their lack of faith. The hero is the putative moral center of the story, yet the enemy brings the conflict that heroism requires.

POWERLESSNESS AND POWER

In addition to distinguishing different sorts of beings, boundaries are drawn between past and present selves and capacities. The felt need for control makes us root for underdogs in fiction (see Polichak and Gerrig 2002). It must be that much more engaging to imagine the prospects of our gaining power ourselves, in self-narrative.

Power is always relational, in two basic ways. We control or wish to control or influence a particular other or group of others. Also, we aspire to possess more control and influence than we currently do. The underdog story promises a vanquishing of vulnerability. The attraction of such can be understood from a psychoanalytic perspective. Our original experiences of being defenseless and aggrieved occur in infancy. Various complexes that Freud identified stem from infantile encounters with dependence in the family, where we are outmatched by powerful others. We effectively replay the scene in later struggles.

A psychoanalytic perspective is not the only one that makes sense of the continuity and intrapersonal depth of the human pursuit of mastery. Running parallel to the point made earlier about good depending on evil (hence the allure of negativity), the reversal from powerless to powerful is as captivating as it is because it highlights the *rightness* of the hero's struggle. The drama of the underdog story is triggered by the fact that the hero is on the side of justice. Even if no other soul currently recognizes it, the underdog is licensed, by God or moral law, to take the action that he does. The engine of the underdog story is a kind of *power paradox*—here, being empowered by some force and yet simultaneously powerless in the present moment (Presser 2013). The struggle toward autonomy has a spirit's blessing.

The struggle endures until the hero triumphs. When triumph is achieved or indicated, the underdog story declares its conclusion. At that point, agency and especially the agency of the enemy is checked. The story sheds its volatility. If a story can be said to have a wish, as is Peter Brooks's (1984) fascinating suggestion, its wish is surely to reach the end when its full meaning is delivered.

PULLING TOGETHER

The plot of underdog stories aligns us with others, though in such a way as to hone our specialness. Aesop's fable "The Lion and the Mouse" foregrounds the element of sociality in the underdog story. In this fable the lion spares the life of the mouse, who later saves the lion, ensnared in rope, from human hunters.

The lesson is not simply that a tiny mouse can triumph, but that mutual aid is the *way* to triumph. By pulling together as a team, we prevail over the mighty adversary. Our strength is in our numbers: so say any number of labor union songs. The underdog story tells us that we are not alone.

Even in stories that have inspired some to what criminologists call lone wolf terrorism, there is a joining with others. Through his solo violent acts, Anders Behring Breivik affiliated with others. His pledge to that effect regularly uses the first-person plural pronoun: "Many brothers and sisters have fallen already, the pioneers, the brave heroes, and the first to pick up their guns. We are the legacy of these first 'unknown' pioneers" (quoted in Berntzen and Sandberg 2014, p. 771). Others situate themselves as front-runners. While Jim David Adkisson, the mass shooter in Tennessee, presented himself as essentially alone in a far briefer manifesto, he connected his actions to those of others to come, stating, "I'd like to encourage other like-minded people to do what I've done" (Knoxnews.com 2009). Adkisson would assume the role of ideological leader, striving toward a collective good. The ends, and not simply the means, are purportedly communal.

That underdog stories appeal in part by their capacity to build collective identity and solidarity is seen by their resonance with other group (e.g., national) myths or master narratives. The American Dream is a version of an underdog story: the hero comes from behind. Commending the film *Rocky* (1976) for its engrossing depiction of the underdog's rise in the boxing ring, Scott Tobias (2015) of *Rolling Stone* magazine quips:

> The challenger [Rocky Balboa] is slow, undersized, and almost perversely unwilling to defend his face or midsection. Were it not for that colorful nickname "The Italian Stallion," Creed would

> have picked some other lethargic bum for a tune-up, sending him back to the Philly ratholes from whence he came. But the 50–1 underdog is both the perfect foil and the true embodiment of the American spirit—all determination and grit. Rocky sends Creed to the canvas with his first punch, the only time the champ has even been knocked out in his career. Yes, our man Balboa loses on points, but the fact that he goes the distance when nobody believed he could suggests a dignity that, say, outslugging Mr. T conspicuously lacks. There are more exciting bouts in the series ... but none that better express the authentic blue-collar toughness at its core.

Rocky's story is one of masculine and specifically white Americanness. Rocky rises, literally and figuratively, against a mythic power-wielding black figure, Apollo Creed, who dominates for a time but is eventually overcome.

In fact, the American story, generally speaking, is deeply unsettled as to the communal life of the protagonist, never abandoning the notion that the hero or anyone else (see Polanyi 1985) is an independent operator. It is best to affiliate but not to enmesh oneself. It is no wonder that *loyalty* is so frequently pledged and performed by the underdog. The concept of loyalty implies voluntary alignment by individuals. The underdog is loyal to his God, nation, leader, or principles.

The underdog's loyalty may be seen as folly by others, and his suffering pathetic, but loyalty and suffering are in fact essential to his eventual triumph. They accentuate the magnitude of his steadfastness. An example from my research comes from Kevin (a pseudonym), who was on death row during our correspondence via phone and mail. In one letter he wrote: "Because of my codes of honor my hands have always been tied. Not to *[sic]* long ago a precious woman I know got on my case about my principles and said things along these lines, what have my codes gotten me, have they kept me warm at night? My principles have gotten me nothing" (Presser 2005, p. 2082). The heroic underdog does sociality by appealing to "higher loyalties" (Sykes and Matza 1957) and ultimately improving the lot of the collective, not (just) his own. That he aspires to achieve that moral feat is evidence of his unusual character.

EVERLASTING MEANING AND MORAL RECOGNITION

Connecting with comrades is just one path to salvation. Connecting with the divine is another, and it is essential. Something construed as crucial and sacred is at stake in underdog stories. The heroic underdog puts everything on the line for something bigger than himself. The significance of the fight lives for posterity. The promise of life beyond loss and death beckons, hence stories that encourage terrorist involvement emphasize martyrdom. The underdog enterprise gives the lives of recruits, to terrorism or any other mass violence, everlasting significance. Recruitment to underdog enterprises extends the promise of meaning (Lyons-Padilla et al. 2015).

Halverson, Goodall, and Corman (2011) describe the Battle of Karbala story popular with Shiite extremist groups: "The conflict between good and evil mediated by a hero accepting his destiny as an archetypical martyr for God's cause is therefore only satisfied by standing against an oppressor and accepting death in defiance of tyranny" (pp. 92–93). Thus, even when he does not achieve the particular earthly goal he had set out for himself, the hero achieves eternal standing. He becomes a durable model of heroism. The story's emphasis is on living (in the beyond) and not dying.

A key dimension of the promise of transcendence is the promise of recognition—of how people and events shall be known. In rousing stories it is not only events that take a dramatic turn: it is also awareness. The dramatic story and especially the underdog story occasions a shift in understandings. The underdog story includes three moments of mis/understanding: broad public misrecognition, the hero's special recognition of the truth, and the public's awakening to the truth.

First, public misrecognition is essential to the drama. The underdog is misunderstood or underestimated early in the story. For example, the expectation prevails that the underdog will be defeated because he is weaker or outnumbered. Others have misjudged his true potential. They may also doubt the worthiness of his cause. Public misrecognition may derive from deception by wrongdoers (see Halverson, Goodall, and Corman 2011, pp. 184–85). Foes commonly seem to be friends: at the least they seem benign. In religious underdog stories, false deities or prophets dupe the people.

Next, the hero grasps the truth of things. The hero knows that his deity is the only true one, that his path is the righteous one. Whereas he sometimes succumbs to doubt, especially self-doubt, he rather quickly returns to his convictions. Or, he sees through some ruse others do not: he has a bad feeling about the deceiver that no one else shares, or no one else will listen. The hero also knows the right moment for action. He is God's confidant who recognizes, for example, God's warning signs for the apocalypse (Mason 2002). His moral distinction translates, among other things, into superior insight.

Lastly, the public awakens to the fact that the hero has been right and righteous all along. This final awakening delivers the transcendent appeal of the story, for the hero-underdog will be known singularly forevermore. He will be the very symbol of heart, determination, and courage. It is telling that the David and Goliath story concludes with an extended discussion of the identity of the heroic underdog—more precisely, befitting the times, the identity of his father (1 Samuel 17: 55–58):

> As Saul watched David going out to meet the Philistine, he said to Abner, commander of the army, "Abner, whose son is that young man?"
>
> Abner replied, "As surely as you live, Your Majesty, I don't know."
>
> The king said, "Find out whose son this young man is."
>
> As soon as David returned from killing the Philistine, Abner took him and brought him before Saul, with David still holding the Philistine's head.
>
> "Whose son are you, young man?" Saul asked him.
>
> David said, "I am the son of your servant Jesse of Bethlehem."

David's actions yield the ultimate prize—individual recognition.

THE GENDER OF UNDERDOG STORIES

The protagonists of underdog stories are most often men, which is the reason I took the liberty of using masculine pronouns throughout this chapter. Why men? After all, women are denigrated and minimized, and they too stand up to their doubters and oppressors. But underdog stories in which women are the primary protagonists are not canonical in most cultures in the way that stories of men are. What might the male-gendered nature of underdog stories have to do with narrative arousal?

The underdog fights; he demonstrates courage; he provides moral leadership; and he has a transcendent, as opposed to a particularistic, moral vision—all of which are associated with men and masculinity (Gilligan 1982). Being down is, in effect, a platform for performing masculinity (C. West and Zimmerman 1987). It is not surprising that the stock-in-trade of sports broadcasting is the underdog story, athletics being a prototypically male domain. In the athlete-as-underdog story, the character of the immoral other is often missing, though one's "own demons"—often self-doubt or drug addiction—fill in nicely.

The underdog's moral accomplishment is burnished if he sought to protect feminized victims and succeeds in doing so. But even without women to protect—daughters, mothers, sisters, motherlands, and so forth—the heroic underdog's accomplishment is meaningful within a context of gender relations (Connell 1995). At the least, the underdog story involves a falsely subordinated masculinity opposing and triumphing over a falsely dominant one. The underdog story might be considered a male fantasy. But it is also a collective fantasy for many people in gender-traditional societies. The fact that the underdog is male hones the power paradox. It heightens the tension between rightful mastery and present subordination. Man down, especially white man down (see L. West 2017), is culturally recognizable as an unacceptable, even illicit state of affairs, which thus provides a basis for an engaging moral reversal.

CHAPTER SUMMARY

Seductive stories channel hopes of achieving control relative to either previous levels or the might of adversaries or both. Underdog stories in particular showcase the spectacular capacity of power positions to turn. The feelings these stories nurture are potential mechanisms of mass harm and especially mass violence.[1]

The heroic underdog puts everything on the line for something bigger than himself and triumphs in this world and in the infinite world. Underdog stories thematize the protagonist's power and position relative to a fierce other *and* relative to the protagonist's current state. The protagonist is physically or logistically less mighty than his adversary. He is physically weak, lacking in adequate resources, but his moral strength—faith, honor, and so forth—will generate the resources he needs for the win. The hero may seem early on to be pitiful, but he is on the side of—indeed, a front-runner of—a righteous cause, often that of God. In addition, the heroic quest constructs groups of loyalists. As such, the story unites us with others and reassures us that we are not alone even through our most challenging missions. In effect, the story resolves the conflict between the desire for distinction and the desire for connection.

The heroic triumph in the underdog story occasions a shift from public misrecognition to recognition. The underdog is underestimated; he alone sees things clearly; finally, others recognize his moral greatness. Being known in that way is his ultimate reward. He and his actions acquire transcendent significance.

CHAPTER FIVE

Becoming a Criminal

A Hegemonic Story of Antisociality

I want to show how stories can drive harm via feeling, but not just so-called violence and not just intense feeling. Stories govern the American criminal justice system and the millions of people under its control. These stories sponsor a web of penal harms (Clear 1994)—detention and imprisonment, solitary confinement, execution, inadequate health care, sexual and other physical victimization, labor for negligible pay, derailed occupational and educational trajectories, political disenfranchisement, destabilized communities, dissolution of families, disentitlement of public benefits, lifelong surveillance, and more. The standard theme of these stories is good thwarting evil. A variety of stories deploy the standard theme. This chapter considers one such story as recounted by a leading theory of criminal behavior, the so-called general theory of crime, and investigates its emotional impact.

The general theory (GT) that Gottfredson and Hirschi (1990) present in their book *A General Theory of Crime* elaborates a popular wisdom concerning criminality—that individuals become criminals through inadequate self-control that stems from inadequate parenting. The core proposition of the GT is that self-control is a foundation for proper conduct, and deficient self-control therefore increases the likelihood of all manner of improper conduct. My examination of the GT is meant to illuminate how some stories may induce a *mood of satisfaction*, which in turn fosters broad backing for harm. Such stories halt volatility and emphasize our own transcendent agency.

This chapter deconstructs the GT's story of antisociality in order to explicate its likely emotional impact. I infer the mollifying impact of the theory on the evidence that most of us tolerate and relatively few protest the penal harm regime it supports. Most of us endorse punishment for some people (see, e.g., Roberts and Hough 2005).[1] Admittedly, my inference makes the analysis speculative. However, I have interviewed persons in the relatively punitive United States who vary in enthusiasm for punishment and criticism of the criminal justice system, and I have almost exclusively encountered in the unenthusiastic or critical camp persons who are also somewhat complacent toward the status quo. Ill will is not necessary for passively abiding by institutionalized criminal sanctioning. This analysis also rests on reflection on when and why I am as complacent as my research participants, despite my experience, expertise, and introspection.

Gottfredson and Hirschi contrast antisocial and prosocial types of people, as well as government and citizenry, and careless and attentive parents. The story's moral oppositions rest on historically specific erasures along lines of gender, race, and class. Other theorists tell stories of antisociality with more dramatic rhetoric concerning the dangers posed by those who undermine and those who preserve peace and order. Before turning to the GT and kindred perspectives, I evaluate satisfaction by way of cognitive theories of emotion. Our emotional reactions to circumstances and incidents track enculturated evaluations of who is influencing our well-being and how successful we are in managing these influencers.

THE CRIMINOLOGIST AS STORYTELLER

The GT is a particular perspective within sociological criminology whose broad project is to clarify the social bases of instances and patterns of offending and criminalization. The theory has received a great deal of attention from American scholars, as evidenced by the amount of research it has stimulated (Pratt and Cullen 2000). Students of the theory include critical criminologists who take it as a singular instance of the essentializing tendencies of mainstream criminology.

I take the GT and all other theories to be stories whether or not they are explicitly presented as such.[2] Theories are time-ordered tellings of things that happen. However much the telling consists in independent and dependent variables and conditioning factors, measured at one point in time, these are temporally staged (first one thing, then another). The variables get worked into a plot, where events and circumstances pre-offense, which amount to causes, result in offending. Both stories and theories make a point. They make meaning out of events, and they assign moral positions to individuals and groups. Theories of crime and theories of harm generally make the point that some illegal or harmful phenomenon is aberrant and should and could be regulated.

Theories have characters—their main agents—like stories do. Some characters, especially protagonists and antagonists, are more important to the plot than are others. Yet, some characters are barely sketched despite their importance (e.g., often, God). Scholars beginning with Aristotle have subordinated character to plot, yet characterization is a mainstay of traditional studies of narrative impact. We identify and empathize with some characters and not with others. Generally, though not always, we relate to villains less than we do to others (see Hogan 2003). The villain of most criminological theories is the offender. Critical criminologists like myself generally avoid vilifying offenders. Yet, we tend to follow along with the mainstream binary of offenders and nonoffenders. We typically use "offender" (versus "victim") terminology and write as though our audience consists of "nonoffenders." I have a place in the telling of a story that contributes to the differentiation of persons.

A MOOD OF SATISFACTION

Emotion scholars devote most of their attention to the so-called primary or basic emotions—happiness, sadness, anger, fear, and disgust (Ekman 1992; Johnson-Laird and Oatley 1989; cf. Ortony, Clore, and Collins 1988). These emotions appear to be universal (Fehr and Russell 1984; Sauter et al. 2010). They tend to produce discernible physiological reactions and recognition on the part of the individuals experiencing them. To a lesser degree, persons in close proximity to those individuals can readily gauge them, as emotions tend to be associated with some sort of bodily (e.g., facial, vocal) signal.

Not surprisingly, researchers have considerably less to say about muted emotional states such as irritation, which is related to disgust, and satisfaction, which is related to happiness. In addition to being more muted than basic emotions, these emotional states may take root gradually, and they may last for a while. Ekman (1992) points to quick onset and brief duration as characteristic of emotion, though he allows that both criteria may be violated. While emotion usually entails cognitive and physical awareness, even to the point of distraction, it need not, as Oatley (1992) observes: "A fully developed, typical emotion ... will have a tone that is experienced consciously and it will include accompaniments of conscious preoccupation, bodily disturbance, and expression. It will also issue in some course of action prompted by the emotion. In certain episodes of emotion, however, an eliciting condition, a feeling tone, some of the accompaniments, or an action consequence may not occur or may not be noticed" (p. 21). Likewise, Ortony, Clore, and Collins (1988) observe that emotions are "internal, mental states that vary in intensity" (p. 13). Whereas these emotion scholars allow a space for low-intensity emotions, it is safe to refer to *moods*, which are taken to be less vibrant and more enduring than an emotion (see Ekman 1984) and to count satisfaction as one such mood.

A mood of satisfaction is a sense of well-being, but a more or less modest one that we might not signal to others or even to ourselves. Satisfaction is roughly equivalent to gratification or comfort. One may consider a spectrum of such positive emotional states, from pleasure to slightly-better-than-neutral acceptance. For example, one might feel "pleased" knowing that one has done a good job, and one might feel "comfortable" knowing that one's partner cheated only once. The latter feeling lines up with the thought and expression "I can live with that." Therefore, at one of its outer limits, satisfaction can approximate Merton's (1938) notion of ritualism, which involves acquiescence to a suboptimal situation.[3] The mood of satisfaction is built on a sense of things as more or less all right with the world. As seen in earlier chapters, stories hone identities. Satisfying stories need not make us look good, but they are the most self-enhancing way of making sense of the world currently available.

In probing satisfaction in the face of harm, we get a handle on harms that hardly inflame those who do not directly suffer from them. They are our business as usual, a backdrop to other activities. The inquiry into the storied grounds of satisfaction heeds Calhoun's (2001) counsel that we not "see emotions only in connection with disruptions to social life" (p. 54). Indeed, "everyday maintenance of social structures" is "equally a matter of emotions" (p. 54).

HIGH STAKES, RHETORICAL RESTRAINT

For some scholars, stories are essentially about high-stakes action, or "the challenges and triumphs of their protagonists" (Nabi and Green 2015, p. 138). Ricoeur (1984) observes: "In the final analysis, narratives have acting and suffering as their theme" (p. 56). Nabi and Green (2015) state: "Narratives, by their nature, are well suited to promote emotional shifts in audiences as they are designed to allow audiences to follow characters through a progression of events that involve facing and often overcoming adversity" (p. 143). Yet, other narrative scholars call attention to the truncated or barely alluded-to story that may concern no one obvious thing (e.g., Bamberg and Georgakopoulou 2008; Hollway and Jefferson 2000). Surely drab or thin stories still qualify as stories. I wade into this dispute because of how a technical story might present only minimally as a story due to the teller's practiced rhetorical restraint.

As seen earlier, the ambit of a story and its stakes are not bound to the apparent triviality or paucity of content. Leaving content sparse or ambiguous leaves doors to reinterpretation and revision open. Figurativeness invites the ingress of weighty experiences recalled from long ago. Also, we very often communicate about big concerns with small rhetorical moves. I found that power was thematized during interludes of seemingly inconsequential chat in story-generating interviews with men who had perpetrated serious violence (Presser 2005). Kevin, who was on death row and soon would be executed, developed a sentimental story of our relationship through our phone interviews and letters. Some of the story's most memorable elements were tropes (Sandberg 2016), such as this prompt to relationship-building: "So I guess you didn't like what I wrote in that letter?" The small story, from this perspective, may actually signify something big, in this case a brash masculinity (he told the brutal truth in that letter) and a tragic romance.

The stories told in social theories are not actually "small"—and often the opposite is true. Rather, they are presented unobtrusively, tending not to call themselves stories. (Another way of saying the same thing: theorists tend not to be reflexive.) Often, though not always, theory-stories erase suffering. They generally avoid emotion terms. In criminological theories the rhetoric is mild but drama is high inasmuch as people are bad or becoming so, to our peril. Emotion terms are not used, although the plotline should, logically, stimulate. Hence a paradox I will now attempt to explain.

THE GENERAL THEORY

Recall that the central claim of the so-called general theory of crime (Gottfredson and Hirschi 1990) is that low self-control causes crime. The person with low self-control "will tend to be impulsive, insensitive, physical (as opposed to mental), risk-taking, short sighted, and nonverbal, and they will tend therefore to engage in criminal and analogous acts" (p. 90). Acts analogous to crime, which likewise reflect low self-control, include drinking alcohol, smoking cigarettes, gambling, getting into accidents, having unstable employment histories, having unwanted pregnancies, having extramarital sex, failure in school, and having accidents. The opportunity for crime and analogous acts matters. Persons inclined to offend will do so only if the circumstances are right. However, Gottfredson and Hirschi assert that opportunity is omnipresent, so low self-control is the main driver of offending: it is "*the* individual level cause of crime" (p. 232; emphasis in original).

Parents must supervise the child's behavior, recognize deviant behavior when it occurs, and punish deviant behavior. They must do these things within "the first six or eight years of life" (p. 272), after which low self-control becomes a stable trait of the individual. It is then "difficult for subsequent institutions to make up for deficiencies" (p. 107). The older child, adolescent, or adult who has not been adequately socialized is constitutionally prone to behaving badly.

Stated Practical Implications of the Theory

Like all criminological theorists, Gottfredson and Hirschi (1990) discuss the implications of their scholarship for social practice. In this regard they have less to say than most, devoting more attention to what will *not* work based on the GT than on what will. Gottfredson and Hirschi critique both rehabilitation (efforts to treat or correct) and selective incapacitation (the targeting of high-rate offenders for formal control). Concerning the latter, they contend that it is impractical to try to identify high-rate offenders and unethical to spare serious but low-rate (e.g., first-time) offenders penal harm.[4] They also cast doubt on the crime reduction potential of increasing police resources or improving policing strategies, or gun control. They criticize job programs as a means of reducing or preventing crime (Gottfredson and Hirschi 1990, p. 232). Their sole explicit policy recommendation has to do with developing the skill of restraining oneself: "Apart from the limited benefits that can be achieved by making specific criminal acts more difficult, policies directed toward enhancement of the ability of familial institutions to socialize children are the only realistic long-term state policies with potential for substantial crime reduction" (pp. 272–73). The authors do not specify what such policies might consist of, only that they involve teaching "the requirements of early childhood socialization" (p. 269). Effective policies simply "must deal with the attractiveness of criminal events to potential offenders and with child-rearing practices that produce self-control" (p. 274).

Gottfredson and Hirschi's (1990) scant discussion of effective policy paves the way for a program of penal harm. First, they presume that crime control efforts are effective—to a limited extent but effective nonetheless. For example, they state: "Of course, robbery can be reduced by increasing the restraints on people who tend toward criminality" (p. 31). Arguing that crimes depend on more than just low self-control, they write: "They also require goods, victims, physical abilities, and *the absence of threats of immediate punishment*" (p. 177; emphasis added). Second, they see no reason to change the penal harm status quo. At the time that *A General Theory of Crime* was published in 1990, imprisonment in the United States was approaching a historic peak.[5] Gottfredson and Hirschi declare: "We see little hope for important reductions in crime through modification of the criminal justice system" (p. xvi). They could have written that they see little hope in *use* of the criminal justice system, suggesting a disapproval of existing—that is, high—levels of formal punishment: they did not. Whereas Gottfredson and Hirschi devote nearly seven pages of the book to a takedown of selective incapacitation, they say nothing about general incapacitation—a less discerning policy of mass control and the policy we have actually undertaken in the United States. Their sole expression of disapproval of punitive control concerns "jail," which they pan along with other "short-term institutional experiences" (p. 232). Crime fighting, they insist, requires sustained commitment. They are silent on what, as a society, that commitment entails. Their silence serves a narrative plot.

Stories of Criminologists and Crime

Gottfredson and Hirschi's (1990) story of antisociality constructs characters and trajectories that produce coveted identities related especially to the power positions of the authors and their audiences. Actually, Gottfredson and Hirschi tell two stories. In addition to their story of antisociality—a story of offenders and their parents failing at living—they tell an academic, factional story of other scholars failing at theorizing. The factional story establishes the authors as experts and thus functions as self-narrative. The authors are its main protagonists. Its antagonists are (virtually all) other criminologists: "Criminology once had an idea of crime, an idea it lost with the development of the scientific perspective" (p. 14). Implicitly, we readers are the protagonist's helpers, supporting the authors in their quest to attain intellectual mastery (Propp 1968).

The factional story is at first preeminent. The book's preface opens with a reflexive statement that establishes this story's emotional dimension: "We have for some time been unhappy with the ability of academic criminology to provide believable explanations of criminal behavior" (Gottfredson and Hirschi 1990, p. xiii).[6] Several of the book's chapters launch with the next installment of the factional story:

> The classical conception of human behavior, with its emphasis on choice in the service of self-interest, eventually gave way to a positivist conception of human behavior, with an emphasis on difference and determinism. (p. 47)

> After sociological positivism replaced biological positivism as the dominant force in criminology, individual correlates of crime were generally ignored in favor of social variables such as urbanization, class, and culture. (p. 123)

The factional story takes up a good deal of space in the book. Yet, in each chapter it eventually recedes to accommodate the story of antisociality. The factional story becomes a berth for the story of antisociality, a situation that readers will probably recognize as standard academic practice. On the way to advancing some argument, scholars tell the story of their idea coming up against other ideas. What I will tease out next is the alliance between the factional story in criminology and the story of antisociality, which establishes a power matrix that gets under our skin.

Gottfredson and Hirschi's story of antisociality describes persons who were not parented correctly in early childhood and are criminally inclined forevermore. Crime follows from "human nature" (Gottfredson and Hirschi 1990, p. 5); the criminal's nature has been allowed to persist unimpeded. The characters of the story of antisociality are the antisocial individual, his or her parents, the civilized citizenry and the state. The authors and their audience are members of the civilized citizenry, also called *noncriminals* (see, e.g., p. 108). Gottfredson and Hirschi work hard at their project and call attention to their hard work: "We want to understand and appreciate the nature of crime. Such a task is not easy" (p. 15). The cerebral nature of their work is at odds with the physicality of the offender's pursuits. Crimes involve physical prowess (e.g., agility) but not much strategy (p. 89). The authors' mathematical precision concerning child development—codified by an unsubstantiated assertion that self-control must be inculcated within "the first six or eight years"—also signals their assiduousness. At various points they send signs of taking great care with inferences, however fictional their empirical bases: "Because crimes tend to combine immediate benefit and long-term cost, we are careful to avoid the image of an offender pursuing distant goals" (p. 114).

Like the authors, we in the civilized citizenry are a conscientious bunch, applying ourselves to interests and concerns beyond immediate pleasure, such as theory and policy. (We are, after all, reading Gottfredson and Hirschi's lengthy book.) We are drastically different from criminals. We have projects, whereas they act based on the whim of the moment. That offenders have no interests and concerns is seen in various dismissals. Crime has "no larger purpose," and offenders "do not have overwhelming impulses to commit crime" (Gottfredson and Hirschi 1990, p. 256). Hyperbolic qualifiers ("larger," "overwhelming") mitigate the harshness of the reduction while they effectively jettison the possibility that offenders invest in anything at all.

All we need to know about offenders can be read off of crime. Crime, according to Gottfredson and Hirschi (1990), is "largely petty, typically not completed, and usually of little lasting or substantial benefit to the offender" (p. 21). The authors explain:

> Our theory was in part devised by working back and forth between an image of crime and an image of criminality. Because crimes tend to combine immediate benefit and long-term cost, we are careful to avoid the image of an offender pursuing distant goals. Because crimes tend to be quick and easy to accomplish, we are careful to avoid the image of an offender driven by deep resentment or long-term social purposes. Because crimes tend to involve as victim and offender people with similar characteristics, we are careful to avoid the image of an offender striking *out* against class or race enemies. (pp. 114–15)

From the outset the authors deny the socially variable and contingent nature of crime.[7] To channel Barthes's (1957, p. 141) thinking on a typical bourgeois maneuver, Gottfredson and Hirschi make Nature out of History. The fiction of the offender's essence builds from there. Nowhere do Gottfredson and Hirschi report what offenders themselves say, from either primary or secondary data. Their images of crime and criminality govern what they know of the offender, such as that the offender cannot possibly care much about injustice: "The notion of inequity at the point of crime is ... incompatible with the image of the offender at the point of criminality" (p. 114). At points, instead of referring to *people* prone to crime, Gottfredson and Hirschi refer to crime, although the result is syntactically awkward: "From classical thought, we derived a theoretical image of crime that turned out to be remarkably consistent with data on actual criminal acts. This image stressed simplicity and the immediate gratification of universal desires, with little concern for long-term consequences" (p. 273). Offenders are treated, linguistically, as vessels of badness, as in the assertion that "so many social problems and forms of deviant behavior are concentrated in the same individuals" (p. xv). The tautology that bothers many critics about the GT (see Akers 1991; Geis 2000;

Hirschi and Gottfredson 2000) effects a saturated criminal identity. The criminal *is* criminality: criminality is the criminal's being as the theorists imagine it. For Barthes (1957), tautology "creates a dead, a motionless world" (p. 153), here a dead and motionless antagonist as well.

Careless Mothers, Strict Fathers, Bad Government

The negligent parent is barely sketched in the story of antisociality. Gottfredson and Hirschi (1990) all but bury the fact that it is mostly women who do the work of child rearing. (That fact appears as parenthetical material on pages 103 and 104.) They pay more attention to the male gender of the likely offender, a fact that itself warrants no special program of research: "As was true of age, gender differences appear to be invariant over time and space" (p. 145). In effect, the authors indict women, particularly minority women (p. 153), for raising delinquent boys. Nothing is new about this formula in criminology (see Hoffman and Vander Ven 2007). What is noteworthy for present purposes is how much it owes for its legitimacy to the effacement of women's *work* and how much *erasures* help to establish the story's legitimacy.

Dorothy Smith (1987), whose method of institutional ethnography investigates the institutional conditioning of social interactions in the everyday, points out the work of inculcating middle-class competencies and the "conceptual strategies that obliterate women as active agents" (p. 164) of that work:

> Somewhere buried in "subcultural process," "social-class attitudes," and the "intricate psychosocial processes of the individual family" is a work organization of families creating the material and moral conditions, the routine order, and the relations with school that concretely accomplish what here is made accountable as school

> achievement and career success. And in this work organization the role of women is central both in the work that is done and in the management of its routine daily order, whether we focus on the provision of conditions under which homework goes forward, the management of relations with school, the work of entertaining, and the like through which the middle-class families socialize children into styles of middle-class sociability, or some other process. Whatever the relation between school achievement, career success, and the "intricate psychosocial processes" of the family, the conscious, planful, thoughtful work of women as mothers has been part of its actuality. But it is not made accountable. (D. Smith 1987, p. 164)

Smith could be describing Gottfredson and Hirschi's or any number of other criminologists' distillation of early socialization. In particular, "intricate psychosocial processes" that go on in the family are utterly disguised as something other than what they are—women's work.

Interestingly, Gottfredson and Hirschi (1990) acknowledge that their vision of anticrime socialization is equivalent to middle-class socialization, stating: "[Albert] Cohen's description of middle-class values ... is a detailed conceptualization of what we mean by self-control" (p. 143). Despite the specificity of values, the work women must do to inculcate middle-class ways of behaving, lest their children become criminals, is not only not made accountable in the book: it is not presented as work. Concern for children morphs naturally into the necessary maneuvers. "The parent who cares for the child will watch his behavior, see him doing things he should not do, and correct him" (Gottfredson and Hirschi 1990, p. 97). In this phrasing "will" guarantees and naturalizes the relationship; Gottfredson and Hirschi might as well be describing the movement of the planets. The authors take advantage of a built-in ambiguity about power and agency which surrounds modal verbs such as will, may, must, and can (Hodge and Kress 1993). The nature of the relationship between caring and the performance of particular tasks is underspecified but vaguely involuntary: correcting simply follows caring. By "care" the authors mean attachment—"parental concern for the welfare or behavior of the child" (Gottfredson and Hirschi 1990, p. 98)—and not labor in the care of the child. "All that is required to activate the system is affection for or investment in the child" (p. 97). Socialization is metaphorically rendered as a mechanical system, where one part activates another without human intervention. Social relationships, feelings, and tutelage of the young are mechanical functions. Why affection and investment are "all that is required" is not explained. The point is that doing the right kind of child rearing is easy and automatic if the mother has the right emotional attitude.

What is at stake in this gendered trivialization of the labors of parenting? As with other mass harm whose narration facilitates the denunciation of victims, *characterizations* are under construction. The parent is someone who could easily redirect her child but does not. She is not someone the civilized citizenry, who, we have already seen, exert effort, can identify with. Nor is she someone who could or would use particular resources (e.g., paid sick leave) to help with raising her children.[8] Her problem is her mind-set. Gottfredson and Hirschi channel storied ideologies of black and poor women with bad attitudes—unnaturally unmotivated to care. Whereas Gottfredson and Hirschi stress that the relationship observed between parents' and children's offending is spurious—that criminal parents are simply more likely to fail as socializing agents—they portray parents as wayward, as themselves probably not well controlled (p. 101). In this way the characterological opposition of "us" and "them" is fortified. The story of antisociality is doubly pathologizing.[9] The criminal has a disorder, and, it is implied, the criminal's parents have one as well.

Gottfredson and Hirschi's story of antisociality maps onto a model of morality that underpins conservative thought, which Lakoff (2002) calls the Strict Father version of morality. Lakoff observes that liberal and conservative American logics correspond to different notions and metaphoric systems concerning the family. It is useful to compare Gottfredson and Hirschi on curbing antisociality with Lakoff on enforcing moral conduct according to Strict Father morality:

> The major cause of low self-control thus appears to be ineffective child-rearing. Put in positive terms, several conditions appear necessary to produce a socialized child.... The minimum conditions seem to be these: in order to teach the child self-control, someone must (1) monitor the child's behavior; (2) recognize deviant behavior when it occurs; and (3) punish such behavior. (Gottfredson and Hirschi 1990, p. 97)

> In short, good parents set standards, good children obey their parents, disobedient children are bad children, good parents punish disobedient children, punishment makes disobedient (bad) children into obedient (good) children, and parents who don't punish are bad parents because they produce bad children by not punishing them when they disobey. (Lakoff 2002, p. 77)

Lakoff (2002) discerns as a main anchor of Strict Father morality the metaphor of Moral Essence, a variant on the Metaphor of Essence according to which people are "objects made of substances that determine how they will behave" (p. 87). The metaphor of Moral Essence states that "past behavior is a guide to essential character and essential character predicts future behavior" (p. 201). Seemingly disparate social issues, including "the role of government, social programs, taxation, education, the environment, energy, gun control, abortion, the death penalty" are "manifestations of a single issue: strictness versus nurturance" (p. x). Strictness is always good for children; brutality is of no concern in this moral worldview. Likewise, Gottfredson and Hirschi (1990) are not alarmed by excessive punishment except insofar as it will not pay off in crime control. Although some parents "are too harsh" (p. 100) others are "too lenient" (p. 100), and both errors arrive at the same result: a probable failure to eradicate the tendency toward bad behavior.

Recall Gottfredson and Hirschi's explicit position that nothing can or even should be done to redirect criminals and their parents. This position is entirely consistent with Strict Father morality as Lakoff (2002, p. 272) describes it: "The mature children of the Strict Father have to sink or swim by themselves. They are on their own and have to prove their responsibility and self-reliance. They have attained, through discipline, authority over themselves" (p. 272). The story constructs grown subjects who are ripe for neoliberalism, obligated to and obligating no one but self. Since Gottfredson and Hirschi developed their theory during the conservative Reagan years in the United States, it is unsurprising to find in the GT story of antisociality strong indications of disapproval of the government. Theirs is "a view in which the state is neither the cause of nor the solution to crime" (Gottfredson and Hirschi 1990, p. 272). They refer to "the relatively weak forces of the criminal justice system" (p. 255), which set up "artificial environments" (p. 269). The story pits government against citizens. Gottfredson and Hirschi "see considerable hope in policies that would reduce the role of the state and return responsibility for crime control to ordinary citizens" (p. xvi). "Policies that would reduce the role of the state" verges on oxymoron, which suggests something incomplete about their disapproval. Indeed, their recommendation of small government sits alongside a tacit approval, discussed earlier, of formal punishment. Logical consistency is no requirement of the impactful story.

Control and Immortality

Whereas in the story of antisociality Gottfredson and Hirschi's tone is bloodless, the story is emotionally consequential. The story maps out not just causality but blame for the criminal and appreciation for the order achieved by the theory (Lazarus 1991). Nussbaum (2001) observes: "Most of the time emotions link us to items that we regard as important for our well being, but do not fully control. The emotion records that sense of vulnerability and imperfect control" (p. 43). Broadly speaking, we experience happy emotions, ranging from intense joy to quiet contentment, when we achieve or possess control over things that matter to us, that are important to our well-being. We experience emotional ease, or a sense of peacefulness and gratification, when the achievement is subtle and measured.

We are powerless before a persistent antisocial nature, as is the antisocial person. We should wield power over such persons. It is our duty to do so and a necessity of collective well-being. We have triumphed over our own nature, and this triumph is inviting as it has to do with personal control. We were at risk of being "powerless in the face of menace—when we should rightly possess (control)" (Presser 2013, p. 108). That is, proper people should possess control, according to dominant American and especially politically conservative models (Lakoff 2002; Polanyi 1985).

The story of antisociality connects to notions of appropriate hierarchies and deviations from them. We are gratified by this story because it sketches a world where our righteous identities are secured. We are like those people Nussbaum (2001) describes as experiencing "joy at their own good character" (p. 42). The story says something about us that we covet, not just that we are good people but that our good personhood is not precarious. In effect, Gottfredson and Hirschi (1990) reassure us that our righteousness will last for a lifetime, grounded as it is on an inherent and immutable orientation. The basis for these beliefs is culturally structured: "When citizens make judgements about who should be included in civil society and who should not, about who is a friend and who is an enemy, they draw on a systematic, highly elaborated symbolic code" (J.C. Alexander 1992, p. 291). The story of antisociality derives from and gives substance to the broader vision and code.

Silence and Indirection

The story of antisociality is built on silences and indirections. We have already discussed the disappearance of women's work and the obliteration of all that is necessary for doing the kind of parenting Gottfredson and Hirschi prescribe to cultivate the noncriminal disposition. It is not surprising, then, that the authors have nothing to say about the social contexts of parenting. They are silent on the necessity of full-time employment that pays enough to meet basic needs, for example, which surely impinges on parents' capacity to pay close attention to their young children. This sort of neglect is par for the course with theories of criminal "processes." The theory is not unusual for occluding a view of societal conditions. What is more deviant, as far as omissions go, is the theorists' uncompromisingly narrow inventory of criminals and crimes.

Gottfredson and Hirschi (1990) reject as an impossibility antisocial conduct perpetrated by a person who in many ways manifests high self-control—someone who has toughed it out through years of schooling, who has put off frivolous fun to build a career, who has abided by most of the laws and norms of everyday life but has overseen or committed violence against the environment, workers, consumers, or family. Agents of harm are never careful or self-regulating. Because criminals are constrained by low self-control in *all* spheres of life, Gottfredson and Hirschi insist on "a relatively low rate of offending among white-collar workers" (p. 191).[10] They do not take on misconduct that is engineered by businesses or governments—as opposed to individual "workers." The state may be inept, but it is no offender. Relatedly, Gottfredson and Hirschi are solely concerned with acts, not patterns; they look past mass harms because crime is "largely petty, typically not completed, and usually of little lasting or substantial benefit to the offender" (p. 21). A drone strike, botched surgery, or an oil spill would not interest them. The authors also reject the idea that collaboration leads to crime, which they discuss under the heading of organized crime. They state that "the idea of crime is incompatible with the pursuit of long-term cooperative relationships, and people who tend toward criminality are unlikely to be reliable, trustworthy, or cooperative" (p. 213).

Gottfredson and Hirschi declare that they have built their crime theory out of qualities of the criminal subject. Their general position is that they have *discovered* such qualities as opposed to having assigned them to the subject—this despite the fact that they very often refer to "the idea of crime" or "an image of crime." They fail to own these ideas and images (of crime), consistently using definite or indefinite articles rather than personal pronouns. In that way Gottfredson and Hirschi ascribe, as so many of their peers in criminology do, a transcendent reality to crime, from which they reify criminal and noncriminal persons.

OTHER VERSIONS OF THE STORY

Other versions of the story of antisociality have been formulated. Some disagree on the causes of low self-control, for example, stressing genetic inheritance (Wright and Beaver 2005) or intelligence (J. Q. Wilson and Herrnstein 1985). Some point to a broader zone of negligence—the community rather than the family (Kelling and Coles 1996; Shaw and McKay 1942; J. Q. Wilson and Kelling 1982). In the latter, community-oriented theories such as social disorganization theory and the broken windows thesis, communities in general are depicted as both in need of change and changeable, so we might expect nonessentializing stories. In fact, community versions of the story of antisociality also essentialize. They also construct moral characters and especially binary ones. They affirm and fortify a dichotomy between the civilized citizenry and antisocial others. And, like the GT story of antisociality, they support the notion that some persons and groups (e.g., youth) require restraint.

An important example is the broken windows thesis, set out by George Kelling and colleagues and rooted in the observation that offenders make offending decisions based on external indications of neighborhood upkeep. The initial antagonist in the story is the problem person who acts in a disorderly fashion: "Not violent people, nor, necessarily, criminals, but disreputable or obstreperous or unpredictable people: panhandlers, drunks, addicts, rowdy teenagers, prostitutes, loiterers, the mentally disturbed" (J. Q. Wilson and Kelling 1982, p. 30). These problem persons are "a source of fear" for "citizens." The problem persons may not ruin the neighborhood, or not right away. But they may cause a certain "atomization" there. The good people stay off the streets and away from each other, which then invites a "criminal invasion." Gradually, one group of undesirables makes way for another—a more dangerous lot—and the good people go elsewhere. Kelling and Coles (1996) recall an encounter Kelling himself had with a putatively dangerous group outside of a Boston subway station, exemplary of what "we" are up against:

> Upon leaving the station, Kelling stopped and looked at the youths directly, at some length—something he would not have done had the (off-duty police) officers not accompanied him. None of the boys could have been older than thirteen or fourteen, weighed more than 140 pounds, or been taller than five foot three. All were African Americans, dressed identically in a dark sweatshirt with hood up, dark baggy pants, and black sneakers. The bench was at the front of the porch and each youth slouched forward—shoulders hunched over, vulture-like—with hands in sweatshirt pockets. Despite the obvious fact that Kelling's companions were police, the four did not shrink back when observed: they simply stared, eyeing Kelling impassively but menacingly. (pp. 236–37)

The broken windows thesis sends a more rousing message than does the GT story. The precariousness of outcomes is more fully described. The thesis draws on the language of combat, which the GT story does not. Spaces are stolen, battles are waged in the courts, sources of disorder are and must be attacked (Kelling and Coles 1996). Hence the theorists' exhortation to take back the streets, the subway, and so forth. An ordinance in Seattle that sought to prohibit "the obstruction of pedestrian traffic" by the homeless is described in dramatic fashion, with reference to grave dangers: "Even this legislation was not sufficient to stem the increase in disorderly behavior, however, nor the potentially ominous consequences for the university neighborhood, and many feared that it was only a matter of time until Seattle's vibrant downtown community would be destroyed by the increasingly brazen behavior of street people" (p. 215). Closer analysis is warranted, but I venture that a rhetoric of war in a story of antisociality stimulates an even more committed variety of satisfaction that is additionally shaped by fear: we might call it *dedication*. Fear is produced by the storied threat—criminology's bread and butter, the portending crime. Since we "can never be done with" the threat (Massumi 2010, p. 53) in light of its futurity, the story of threat is a reliably renewable source of feeling.

CARING A LITTLE OR NOT AT ALL

We have scrutinized a story that produces widespread tolerance of penal harm. Stories that promote harm in general construct harm targets either as beyond the scope of concern *or* as concerning because they could threaten us (Presser 2013). Caring little about the target's well-being tends to go hand in hand with indifference. Lazarus's (1991) distinction between knowledge and appraisal assists in clarifying indifference from the perspective of emotion theory. Knowledge tells us things, whereas appraisal tells us how those things affect us. An appraisal prompts an emotional reaction when appraisers determine that the cognized event affects their personal well-being. That effect may be strong or weak, which then determines the intensity of the reaction. Lazarus refers to hot versus cold cognition: "Cognition can be relatively cold when there is *minimal self-involvement or low stakes* in what is thought; cognition can also be hot or emotional" (p. 131; emphasis in original). We might experience cold cognition when we assemble knowledge of an event or circumstance and determine that we have little stake in it. If I determine that a story of the killing of journalists in some far-off country does not affect me, I am unlikely to get very emotional: my cognition will remain cool.

Also, we may not care about targets' well-being because those individuals are responsible for the misery that they endure. Even if wronged at some earlier point, they must henceforth "take responsibility" for their actions. Criminals fit this description, as do various others in contemporary neoliberal politics, such as the children of "illegal" immigrants. Women who suffer from abortion and criminal suspects harmed in police custody warrant no compassion for what befalls them. Persons deemed bad clearly deserve the bad things that happen to them. A story in which victims are partly or fully responsible for their suffering should promote indifference though not active harm. The situation, to use Hughes's (1964) words, strikes us as "a little bit too bad" (p. 30).

Other targets, like nonhumans and slaves, may be of minimal concern by virtue of their ascribed identity or constitution. Their characterization is thoroughgoing and less complex than deservingness of suffering implies. Lines from Colson Whitehead's acclaimed novel of 2016, *The Underground Railroad*, showcase, among other emotions, the apathy that precluded recognition of enormous suffering caused by slavery in the United States: "The townspeople looked at the colored girl laying there collapsed on the ground and stepped over her into the bakery. The smell of the snacks filled the street, sweet and beguiling" (p. 208). Contemporary cultures grant *some* consideration for *some* of the suffering of *most* creatures, human and nonhuman. Therefore, those who have a stake in the suffering of others regularly obscure its material reality, such as by physically locating it where it cannot be readily observed by nonvictimized people—would-be interveners. Consequently, few of us hear stories that thematize the suffering. We also miss stories that offer alternative explanations for the social problems that engender it and alternative characterizations of those implicated in and affected by those problems.

Then, we may care a great deal for our own well-being, over which the target potentially has some influence. And still my cognition may be cold. If this threatening target is, in the story that I embrace, under control or fairly controllable, I may feel satisfied by the harm being done. Unlike the hero in the underdog story (chapter 4), the civilized assembly of state, criminologist, and citizen depicted in the story of antisociality is not coming from so far behind. We have resources, and we know it. Yet, our mission is no less important or noble than is that of the underdog hero—to secure safety and establish order. Everything, still, is on the line. The license to exert control on account of the agent's good character adjoins the necessity of doing so on account of the would-be subject's bad character.

We may situate the mood of satisfaction historically, as Jock Young (2011) does: "In order to tackle ontological insecurity people look for fixed categories and essences, definitions of themselves and, very importantly, in order to validate those definitions, clear images of others, delineated from themselves. Thus the popular need, in late modernity, for clear-cut identities meshes with a science that needs precise delineations" (p. 73). In theorizing crime, especially violent crime, terrorism, genocide, *and* punishment in late modernity, Young (2003) observes that "much of the dynamic behind crime is resentment and much of the response to it is vituperative" (p. 391). How shall we reconcile the buzzing insecurity and anger that Young (2003, 2011) describes with Foucault's instrumentalist orientation toward punishment (see also Feeley and Simon 1992)? In my view we are today resolute in stigmatizing and yet comforted that the project of dealing with those we stigmatize is being well taken care of, in terms of both theorization and practice. Then, what looks like civilization to Elias (2000) may simply be outsourcing and institutionalization. We have offloaded jurisdiction over safety concerns onto others, whether individual "pariahs who do the dirty work of society" in the context of Nazi Germany (Hughes 1964, p. 30) or mechanized systems that operate out of sight. Clearly, strong emotion promotes an enthusiasm for punishment (Johnson 2009), yet I maintain that less passionate moods promote support as well. My argument in effect has been that complacency with penal harm depends just as much as harm by one's own hand on deep cultural meanings (see P. Smith 2008).

FERTILE GROUND: STORY RECEPTION

Social and economic conditions prime audiences to hear a story. The story resonates with what is going on. Crime in general and violent crime in particular were peaking at the time of the publication of *A General Theory of Crime* (see, e.g., Cooper and Smith 2011). That would explain active storytelling about crime, but why *this* story? The likelihood of audience response is increased when new stories "conform to stories we have heard before" (Polletta 2006, p. 169). Fisher (1987) observes: "We ask whether or not an account is faithful to related accounts we already know and believe" (p. 194). Active authorial strategies for enhancing believability thus include connecting the new story to cultural narratives that are generally accepted as true. The GT and stories like it are consistent with dominant stories not only about criminals but also about racial minorities. All the better that those stories are rendered color-blind for a post–civil rights era white public (Bonilla-Silva 2017). Much depends, too, on the resources of storytellers, for "configurations of power and resources determine what kind of a hearing particular stories secure" (Polletta 2006, p. 167). The status of the authors of the GT was high, as were its outlets—a prestigious university press and prominent journals. Conditions were right for learned men to augment the canon of stories of problem persons.

CHAPTER SUMMARY

We should probe the emotional experience of stories that lure us on board with the projects they configure—perhaps with the mildest of felt investment. That was my purpose here, to clarify the muted emotional mechanics of narratives that sponsor pain-causing public policy. This chapter deconstructed one criminological theory-cum-story that animates contemporary criminal justice in the United States. It contributes to an entrenchment of criminal justice institutions and ideologies, and operates cognitively and affectively. It is crucial that we discern the artful practices of criminological theories because they steer public policies that cause harm, and they nurture consent for those policies.

A factional story, in which Gottfredson and Hirschi (1990) contest the standard ideas of criminology, was shown to be a conduit for telling a story of antisociality. The factional story sets out who the storytellers are within their social field. It is one identity statement; the story of antisociality is another. The story of antisociality is an identity vehicle for the good people among us. First and foremost it addresses our need for agency and control. If we cannot be assured of safety from antisocial others, we can at least be assured that they are being called out and, on that basis, tracked down. It also supplies a framework for self-recognition as virtuous, telling us that we, like the authors, are proper people (Polanyi 1985). Our virtue becomes part of us and is enduring. Hayden White (1975) observed that the theorizing of the historian is "little more than a formalized projection of qualities assigned to the subject in his original figuration of it" (p. 54), thereby tying theory to characterization and emphasizing the scholar's active part in the latter. Gottfredson and Hirschi say that theirs is a particular figure ("idea") of crime but proceed to treat crime as an objective phenomenon that follows from objective (and ultimately permanent) states of individual being. A mood of satisfaction is the result of a neat bifurcation of noncriminals whose actions matter and will stand the test of time, and criminals whose actions are of no consequence.

As Barthes (1957) said of myth, the story of antisociality "abolishes the complexity of human acts, it gives them the simplicity of essences, it does away with all dialectics, with any going back beyond what is immediately visible, it organizes a world which is without contradictions because it is without depth, a world wide open and wallowing in the evident, it establishes a blissful clarity" (p. 143). The story of antisociality operates in essential ways through erasures—of most of what "offenders" and their earliest caregivers have going on in their lives, and most of what caregiving and living and transgressing actually entail. Intentions are whittled down or denied, including the fact that transgressors have any intentions at all.

The story casts tellers the way they would like to be (or do not mind being) cast, and casts others so as to support those preferred identities. But not just goodness, also its everlastingness, is created out of the story of antisociality. This vision of immortal goodness contributes to a sense of satisfaction, which is fuel for penal harm.

CHAPTER SIX

Better Living in Story Worlds

> The recipe for populism is universal. Find a wound common to many, find someone to blame for it, and make up a good story to tell. Mix it all together. Tell the wounded you know how they feel. That you found the bad guys. Label them: the minorities, the politicians, the businessmen. Caricature them. As vermin, evil masterminds, haters and losers, you name it. Then paint yourself as the savior. Capture the people's imagination. Forget about policies and plans, just enrapture them with a tale. One that starts with anger and ends in vengeance. A vengeance they can participate in.
>
> Andrés Miguel Rondón (2017)

People and other creatures suffer and die because of stories. It is happening right now. Hence the urgency of narrative criminology and related research programs in other academic disciplines. We need to know more about harm-promoting stories and how they operate.

This book began with the observation that stories do not just tender ways of making situations, individuals, and groups understandable. They do more than guide and condone action. Stories beguile and engross us.

Notwithstanding some excellent research on stories framing mass harm, their affective aspect has been undertheorized, despite the fact that affect in and via narrative is a major focus of literary scholars and others in the humanities, and despite the fact that emotion, including emotional numbness, is a focal theme of important studies of mass harm that do not center on stories (e.g., Arendt 1963; Goldhagen 1996; Scheff 1994). Social researchers agree that something about culturally recognizable plotlines gets us going, that the influence of stories on action is part emotional influence. They have pointed to the affective impacts of stories on collective action without clarifying the nature of such impacts. However, their understanding of arousal processes has been largely intuitive. I have not been satisfied to leave the matter at that. Gamson (1988) powerfully observes: "Every regime has a legitimating frame that provides the citizenry with a reason to be quiescent" (p. 219). Without denying that we do what we do for "a reason," my analysis has, in effect, sought out the affective basis of quiescence and direct action besides.

A vast body of work in the humanities and social sciences led the way. Literary and sociolinguistic scholars tell us about the nature and capacities of narrative. Philosophers consider what an aesthetic state of mind is; communication scholars ask what about a form induces it. Psychologists illuminate immersion in stories, identification with story characters, and provocation by figurative speech. Experts on emotion supply insights on processes of emotional response. This book has started the work of connecting these and other intellectual reservoirs patently concerned with transgression, especially cultural sociology and cultural criminology, to arrive at a theory of narrative incitement leading to active and passive harm.

In this concluding chapter I will summarize my main insights—concerning how narrative generates emotional force, why some narratives are especially forceful, and why so-called drama is not necessary for impact. Then, I want to take this space to contemplate a thorny issue for social research into narratives—what textual form impactful narratives take. Finally, I will set out what I see as promising interventions, for the sake of better living in the story worlds we inhabit.

THE AROUSAL POTENTIAL OF NARRATIVE

Stories are unique among discursive forms for the unifying common sense they provide, the volatile agency they tend, and the explanatory work they do. These capacities contribute to feeling insofar as feeling arises from evaluations of the world as these bear on precarious well-being, moral identity, and control. Narratives arouse us inasmuch as they portray physical and spiritual being in flux. They comfort us when they portray "being" as we wish it to be.

The Past and Future in the Present

The audience to stories, Maan (2015) reminds us, is active: "The audience will put together elements of the message that cohere with the story they are a part of and either disregard or react against elements that don't cohere with the story the audience is a part of" (p. 64). How we react to texts or anything else partly depends on earlier experiences that we have internalized (Nussbaum 2001), which lurk as memory traces (Hogan 2003).[1] Hence Lazarus's (1991) explanation of how "instantaneous appraisals" may be "made in response to minimal clues": those "appraisal patterns have, as it were, already been set in advance" (p. 151). The notion of preformed appraisals is compatible with that of narrative habitus, which Fleetwood (2016) defines as "the internalisation of the narrative doxa pertaining to the field, including vocabulary, narrative formats, tropes, discursive formats and subject positions etc." She notes that "narrative doxa pertaining to fields structure how stories are received, including notions of truth" (p. 181). Our internalized ways of storying a situation fast-track present understandings and hence feeling. However much they are embodied, they are also profoundly socialized.

But stories do not merely connect the past with the present. Stories also reach forward in time. They gesture at what will or should prevail in the future. In the more or less far-off future, of course, we will all be dead. Stories suggest meaning beyond that time (Becker 1973; Frankl 1984)—meaning that transcends time, hence stories' ultimate emotional freight.

Moral Oppositions and Identity Statements

Some narratives are more impactful than others because they instate the moral oppositions and make the identity statements that we favor or at least accept, such as concerning our position vis-à-vis others. They install culturally familiar and rewarding versions of ourselves and our lives. Two dimensions of the drawing of moral boundaries, and thus selves, emerged from my analysis. First, negativity and stark contrasts, such as between honorable and evil, are especially enticing—foundationally so, it seems. We enjoy discord and disapproval. That regrettable human tendency is partly—but only partly—responsible for the gratification we feel in "knowing" that offenders are constitutionally bad. That "knowledge" illuminates our own moral distinction besides. Second, we may not particularly like or benefit from our current storied identities, but they serve us as well as or better than any other identities we can fathom given our social and cultural location.

With or without Drama

The phenomenon of narrative transportation seems not to depend on a specific story or genre, as Gerrig (1993) notes: "We can see that no a priori limits can be put on the types of language structures that might prompt the construction of narrative worlds" (p. 4). The example of underdog stories engendering terrorism and other mass violence highlights the frisson stimulated by extreme moral and material contests and reversals. The example of stories of antisociality supporting penal harm brought to light the more subdued but no less "emotional" acceptance provoked by stories that lack drama because they pit us versus them in less inflammatory terms, but that still score a win for certainty, control and transcendent being.

Stories we find minimally "acceptable," which nonetheless deliver an emotional charge, tend to operate under the radar and thus go unnoticed.[2] They seem not to stir us at all, although stories meant to subvert those usually hegemonic tales often draw ire. They provoke satisfaction rather than apathy. Satisfaction is an emotional state not much explored in the literature on narrative impacts, being more likely to attract scholarly cynicism—say, regarding audience preferences for full resolution of conflict and happy endings—than serious inquiry. Yet, the fact that emotions "override other concerns, other goals, and other actions," according to Frijda (1988), "applies to action as well as to nonaction, to fear's impulse to flee as well as to grief or despair's lethargy" (p. 355). Stories give comfort to bystanders when others are suffering, by telling us those others are unimportant or deserving of their pains. Stories also satisfy because they position us favorably relative to social or moral inferiors, often through conventional omissions and silences.

WHAT KIND OF TEXTS ARE NARRATIVES?

Throughout this book I have emphasized narratives as linguistic entities. I have put narratives in league with figures of speech. Here and there I have analyzed the wording of consequential narratives. But our most prototypical stories have no single textual existence. These are among the most pervasive and influential stories in a society, so it is important to consider how they function.

I conceive of two forms of narrative based on their materiality: *bounded narratives*, which are specific texts, and *notional narratives*, which vary from version to version. Bounded narratives have a clear start and ending; we can count their words. Mass shooter Jim David Adkisson recorded a bounded narrative, which the reader can access online (Knoxnews.com 2009). Hitler's *Mein Kampf* is another bounded narrative. In contrast, notional narratives lack a stable textual basis. No single recorded version exists. My own life story is notional to the extent that I tell it differently on different occasions. Notional narratives are like plot summaries. They are sometimes called story genres, templates, or standard plots. They tend to be referenced in shorthand: rags to riches, American Dream, redemption narrative, underdog, and so on. They admit to different versions. An example that literary scholars have scrutinized in depth is the Cinderella story. Even multiple story versions that seem to be "the same" are not written or spoken in precisely the same way from one speaker or one telling to another.

The two forms of narrative are closely related. Notional narratives generally descend from bounded narratives. We might say that they paraphrase bounded narratives. Consider summaries and tweets of a bounded narrative. The different bounded stories of different storytellers in a group are seen to add up (often controversially) to a notional narrative. For example, when enough influential speakers tell a comparable bounded narrative of immigration, we can speak of "the" narrative of immigration. Also, the bounded narrative that resonates with enough people (perhaps at a certain determinable tipping point) is on its way to becoming notional.

In studying narrative impacts, we can examine bounded narratives and grasp something specific to a text—albeit reaching large audiences with widespread implications—or we can examine notional narratives and grasp broader understandings. Both kinds of examinations are important, but I believe that a cultural sociology of contemporary mass harm is in greater need of the latter because the most pervasive and impactful narratives are notional. Even a patently decisive bounded narrative—Hitler's *Mein Kamp* is an example—had its impact via a condensed notional narrative of Germany's degradation. Likewise, today's neoliberal, white supremacist, xenophobic, and pro-terror narratives are widely, globally, and rapidly disseminated mainly in notional form, facilitated by the Internet and social media. In turn, these form convictions about patterns among audiences, striking them as all the more true for being subterranean.

Notional narratives are more likely to be metanarratives (Lyotard 1984), hegemonic stories (Ewick and Silbey 1995), or master narratives (Halverson, Goodall, and Corman 2011). Halverson, Goodall, and Corman (2011) define a master narrative as "a transhistorical narrative that is deeply embedded in a particular culture" (p. 14) and observe that it "can be invoked without actually telling a story" (p. 182). Lyotard's metanarratives and grand narratives and Ewick and Silbey's (1995) hegemonic stories dominate other stories and thereby effect oppression. The concept of notional narrative is more technical than these others. We may speak of the notional narrative disseminated by a marginalized group, concerning their oppression or anything else. Similarly, critical social theories are not hegemonic, though they are notional narratives. Indeed, there is something democratic about the viability of notional narratives. And yet, I venture that notional stories are more likely to become doxa, to use Bourdieu's term. They are shortcuts to deeply rooted emotional-cognitive linkages. People can make notional narratives "their own," as evidenced by highly idiosyncratic—say, theological or intergenerational—but culturally forged accounts of climate change. In short, however much bounded narratives may affect us, notional narratives should act with even greater force.

MAKING CHANGE

Feelings are fundamentally hard to resist. I am not optimistic that we can mitigate the emotional force of stories or interrupt our reactions. Highlighting the emotional aspect of narrative, as I have, in fact reaffirms the power of narrative given the tendency of emotions in general to elude our control (Frijda 1988). In contrast, stories themselves are not irresistible, and this is clear from the simple fact of variation between individuals and in the lives of individuals, even when circumstances are alike. Our needs and wants make certain narratives more attractive than others. We tend to gravitate toward particular stories. Under the dominant cognitive paradigm of psychotherapy today, practitioners help us recognize the stories that we keep casting ourselves in to our detriment and misery. Different narratives appeal to us under different circumstances and at different times and life stages. Appraisals are "continually changing, which is why emotions are always in flux" (Lazarus 1991, p. 134). As such, individuals (i.e., appraisers) bring *themselves* to stories, an idea captured by the concept of *resonance*, which Lazarus calls "an amorphous or ineffable sense of connection between what is in us and something in the outer world" (p. 154). And therefore, after all, there is a self that is separate from the story. That self makes choices. Whereas narratives transport us, they cannot take us to places we do not wish to go. Interventions that clarify the force of both desire and story are essential.

Alas, stories are notoriously difficult to discern in the moment. Nonetheless, I know that I am living inside of a story by reflecting on how I lived inside of my old stories in the past. The obstacles and tormentors set out in those old stories seem patently implausible to me now. It is not simply that the circumstances of my life have changed. The whole saga is foreign; it seems obvious to me that those obstacles and tormentors were not real. But back then, there was a naturalness to the story. It not only seemed true: *it did not seem like a story.*

How can we connect to the self that chooses stories? How shall we free ourselves of stories operating in real time? I believe that we can and should commit ourselves to *two tasks*: resisting harmgenic stories and developing new stories.

Resisting Stories

It takes a critical consciousness to grasp the stories that captivate us at any given moment. To deliberately resist the appeal of a story, it is necessary to secure a space outside of the story, to critically appraise it. Then, we can "question/undermine/deconstruct the authority of the powers that legitimate" the story (Maan 2015, p. 65).

Teachers know that we can hold students accountable only when there is something concrete to account for. Writing the narrative down—getting a handle on it—is a first step toward interrogating it. Then, we can alert would-be recipients to the nature of the problem narrative. For that, I believe, "we need general forums where our harmful actions and arrangements are made perfectly clear, their underlying logics are interrogated, the connections between logics and harms are discerned, and feasible plans are made for change" (Presser 2013, p. 124). Participants in public assemblies about issues of crime, safety, housing, zoning, and health care, for example, can be made aware of the stories they are channeling and telling, whose stories they are, and with what plotting and characterizations.

I have taken specific aim in this book at underdog stories and stories that immobilize character and agency. Many versions of these, from different ends of political spectra, exist in the world. We must take care not to single out particular dangerous narratives and not others. We must take them all into view and furthermore showcase their overarching connections. Grossman (2015) critiques current counternarrative/counterterrorism strategies in the West: "Beyond the need to widen convincingly the discursive net of extremism to include non-neo-jihadi forms of terrorism, contemporary counter-narratives against violent extremism are also failing to address other, critically important social and cultural narratives now besieging many modern democracies.... Moreover, contemporary counter-terror narratives need to avoid undermining their own premises of democratic debate and an open field of ideas and expression by remaining committed, as they still appear to be, to the rigid binarisms of 'Islamic' versus 'Western' regimes of value and meaning" (p. 76).

In order to resist harmgenic stories, then, we take the full measure of them and the stories, including "past" stories, they connect to. We should be reflexive and self-searching, always asking which understandings we have taken to be self-evident and which understandings we have left out. We should forcefully acknowledge, for example, that *we* have hierarchized harm projects, that *we* channel the stories that reproduce the hierarchies and the stories that animate them.

Telling Different Stories

In addition to questioning current stories, we must generate and disseminate counternarratives.

Stories are interdiscursive; they borrow from or connect with other stories. The young Somali-Canadians interviewed by Joosse, Bucerius, and Thompson (2015) interpreted and rejected the (storied) recruitment efforts of al-Shabaab in terms of a boogeyman narrative. Several men with violent histories whom I interviewed told stories of being silly, incompetent criminals (Presser 2008). They used comic narratives to oppose the "absolutization of character" (Hogan 2003, p. 214) heavily emphasized in stories of antisociality.

The project of counternarration is fraught with risk, as Grossman (2015) has shown in regard to doing counterterrorism. It is vital that counternarratives emerge among those who might succumb to the harm-promoting stories, as in the examples just mentioned. We must also take care that counternarratives are true stories, such as I have previously described (Presser 2013): "The characters in true stories are ever on their way to becoming something else. This is the case—it is at least hinted at—even when the storyteller pronounces the story's end. For the sake of unmaking misery, it is particularly important that storytellers acknowledge the dynamism of living. We have seen how target reduction freezes who the target—and often too the speaker—is. True stories suggest variable personifications, readings, twists, and endings. We also saw the dangers in claiming both power and powerlessness. True stories feature more authentic appraisals of one's capacities and incapacities" (p. 123).

My designating complex stories as "true" is meant to be provocative given problematics confronted earlier. I conceive of truth as continuous, not binary, and as something we continually advance. The true story opens the possibility of alternative resolutions and perspectives. It is full of surprises save one—that our time is limited. Baroni (2015) proposes that "it is only because we don't know with total certainty how the story will end that we can engage in a free and responsible act of any kind" (p. 51). Closure is a myth we would do well to question whenever it is summoned.

Just as storying the Other and the situation in a particular instance might have fostered (or be fostering) harm, so can storying figure into helping. Nussbaum (2001) observes that "the imagination is a bridge that allows the other to become an object of our compassion" (p. 66). Stories effect change and resistance against harm (J.E. Davis 2002; Ewick and Silbey 1995; R.N. Jacobs 2002; Polletta 2006). After a particular harmful action has been perpetrated, a great many stories are told—in the news, on social media, by scholars, in formal legal arenas, and so on. Restorative justice in the aftermath of a crime or other conflict aims both to heal harms and to change stories about harming. Storytelling during dialogic sessions of restorative justice, including truth and reconciliation commission hearings and family group conferences, is designed to be less encumbered than in courtrooms and probation offices. Given its emphasis on harm and healing, "restorative justice can encourage the telling of true stories, where the message surfaces that we all play a part in harm. Another potential message of restorative justice encounters is that none of us wishes to harm per se. Both of these messages can unsettle notions of who we and others are" (Presser 2013, p. 125).

Restorative justice is a concept that informs responses to harm even without a victim-offender encounter. It extends to "instruments such as an Environmental Victims Charter that speaks of repairing the harm and ensuring compensation for human and non-human victims of climate change" (R. White and Heckenberg 2014, p. 115). Such instruments are narrative tropes (Sandberg 2016), which reflect a newer, truer story of environmental harm that casts a broad global range of both victims and agents of harm. A restorative justice–inspired process aimed at racial reconciliation and reparations for African Americans could generate counternarratives to "the deep story" of American conservatism, according to which whites cannot get ahead because of the privileges bestowed upon others (Hochschild 2016). The new story would highlight webs of institutionalized traumatization in connection with historically complex material and moral positions.

It is noteworthy that restorative justice has been presented as a vehicle for fostering *emotional* change (Braithwaite 1989) and has also been charged with undertaking that task irresponsibly (Van Stokkom 2002). Restorative justice encounters may cultivate counterproductive shame. They may impose certain stories on participants and thus demand certain emotions (e.g., remorse) of them. Notwithstanding its hazards, I find it commendable that planners (and critics) of restorative justice make the links explicit between storytelling, emotional response, and action, when those links have tended to be sidelined just about everywhere else in arenas of justice and social inquiry.

NOTES

CHAPTER ONE. INTRODUCTION

1. For the most part I use the terms *narrative* and *story* interchangeably, following most (but by no means all) of the writers whose work I cite. I define narrative or story as a discursive form that meaningfully recounts some experience, purportedly fictional or hypothetical or real, highly specific and event-bound or wide-ranging.

2. Narrative criminology is also concerned with inhibition of or resistance to harm via stories.

3. A discourse analysis less attuned to linguistic mechanics has also been a destination for thinkers influenced by Michel Foucault.

4. See Eagleton (1991) and Stanley (2015) for comparable claims regarding ideology and propaganda, respectively.

5. Indeed, theories of aesthetic education prescribe artistic appreciation to counteract patterns of injustice (see, e.g., Spivak 2013; Worth 2017).

6. Some fiction casts real-world individuals having not-real-world experiences, such as the film *Being John Malkovich* (1999). Many more fictional stories involve made-up individuals having experiences that

are inspired by real-world events, such as the film *Saving Private Ryan* (1998).

7. The desire to believe the story is one variable that impinges on the timeliness of (say, it might delay) political accountability.

8. There is, in addition, reason to believe that those who are lying to others are also lying to themselves, the latter evidently making them better (i.e., more persuasive) at the former (M.K. Smith, Trivers, and von Hippel 2017).

CHAPTER TWO. THE CULTURAL GROUNDS OF MASS HARM

1. I use the terms *discursive* and *discourse* to refer to language in use. Discourse includes figurative devices, narratives, comments, inventories, labels, buzzwords, articles, and other forms.

2. An alternative focus for criminology, the violation of social norms, is likewise forged from the concerns and definitions of a dominant group, as arbiter of the norms that matter. Only inquiry into harm privileges the perspective of victims.

3. Deindividuation, or loss of self-consciousness, self-restraint, and feelings of individual agency, is a conceivable result (Zimbardo 1970). Against Kelman's (1973) account of the callousness of the functionary, Zimbardo's theory of deindividuation posits that impulsive urges, such as seen in angry crowds, come to reign.

4. Less common are investigations of comprehensive codes that promote harm, such as Klemperer's (2007).

5. The concept of reduction also overlaps with Opotow's (1993) notion of moral exclusion.

6. Nor are nonviolent or just arrangements any less discursively constructed than violent or unjust ones.

7. Breivik killed seventy-seven people in Norway on July 22, 2011, via car bombing in Oslo and mass shooting on the nearby island of Utøya.

8. The Russian formalists distinguished between *syuzhet* (or *siuzhet*) and *fabula*, where *syuzhet* relates the events as told in the text, sometimes called plot, and *fabula* relates the events as they supposedly occur in the world of the characters. The distinction, often taken for

granted, is a point of agreement across a range of literary theories under the rubrics of structuralism and formalism (Culler 2001).

9. Plot and character do most of the moralizing work of narrative (Sternberg 2001). Therefore, it is intriguing to ponder that in addition to their conventional meanings related to narrative, *plot* may be defined as some wicked plan, and *character* may be defined as the sum of a person's qualities; to *have* character is to have specifically admirable moral qualities. The polysemy of plot and character cues us to narrative's moral aspect.

10. Consider arguments that the self-narrative thesis takes as its object only expansive autobiographical accounts and ignores more narrowly focused stories (Bamberg and Georgakopoulou 2008; Hyvärinen 2008).

11. In addition, humanists have both adopted and critiqued this view (see, e.g., Eakin 2006; MacIntyre 1981; Phelan 2005; Schechtman 1997, 2007; Strawson 2004; Taylor 1989).

CHAPTER THREE. EMOTION, NARRATIVE, AND TRANSCENDENCE

1. This idea is versatile, connecting with physiological theories of emotion, such as the influential James-Lange theory, which conceptualizes emotion as the perceived physiological arousal induced by an experience (Lang 1994).

2. Literary scholar James Phelan (1989) uses *completeness* the way I am using *closure*. He explains: "Closure, as I use the term, refers to the way in which a narrative signals its end, whereas completeness refers to the degree of resolution accompanying the closure. Closure need not be tied to the resolution of instabilities and tensions but completeness always is" (pp. 17–18).

3. Some excellent studies of collective memory and the law pertain to mass harm specifically (Minow 2002; Savelsberg and King 2011).

4. Both are taken to be strategic devices used for persuasion. Yet, both ambiguity and figurativeness are conventional. As Culler (2001) writes, the literal use of language is "at best something to be constructed with difficulty" (p. 206).

CHAPTER FOUR. THE INVITATIONAL EDGE OF UNDERDOG STORIES

1. Underdog stories can also arouse opposition to mass harm, as Rob White and Heckenberg (2014) write in regard to environmentalism: "The activist who risks life and limb against the Japanese whaler makes a good and sensational story" (p. 64). I leave for another day (or another researcher) the question of whether the form is itself harmgenic in the long if not the short run.

CHAPTER FIVE. BECOMING CRIMINAL

1. However, in studying the matter, researchers usually take that stance for granted—that people desire punishment for at least some so-called offenders. For instance, Roberts and Hough (2005) remark: "Many public attitudes studies simply give subjects a brief description of a case to consider, and then ask them to impose a sentence from a limited number of dispositions" (p. 79).

2. Postmodernists will have no issue with the view of theories as telling stories. However, that view runs up against a traditional scientific one of theories advancing an objective model of reality based on data. An intermediate position is that theories get communicated aesthetically, rhetorically, and thus often in narrative form. Garfinkel (1967) makes this point: "Every kind of inquiry without exception consists of organized artful practices whereby the rational properties of proverbs, partially formulated advice, partial description, elliptical expressions, passing remarks, fables, cautionary tales, and the like are made evident, are demonstrated" (p. 34).

3. Ritualism is one of five adaptations to societal strain that Merton (1938) identified.

4. "No matter how little risk is posed by them, some first-time offenders must on grounds of justice or deterrence be punished by imprisonment" (Gottfredson and Hirschi 1990, p. 264).

5. The National Research Council reported in 2014 that "the imprisonment rate grew rapidly and continuously from 1972, increasing annually by 6 to 8 percent through 2000" in the United States (Travis, Western, and Redburn 2014, p. 34).

6. The book ends similarly: "In the end, we will be happy if our theory helps renew some intellectual interest in criminology, a field that once engaged the finest minds in the community" (Gottfredson and Hirschi 1990, p. 275). It is noteworthy that the authors use emotion terms in the self-narrative but suppress them in the story of antisociality.

7. Likewise, they reject variation between offenses. Whether they are status offenses, violent offenses, against property or person, instrumental or expressive, crimes are all cast from the same mold (see Gottfredson and Hirschi 1990, p. 44).

8. Note how a story of criminality promotes harm not just to "criminals" but also to their kin, not just via "criminal justice" but through other social policies as well.

9. Maan (2015) writes: "A pathologizing narrative is a narrative with a theme that something is wrong and the thing that is wrong is inside a person" (p. 18).

10. Rather old and sparse research tells them that that low rate is not a result of less attention by the criminal justice system (see Gottfredson and Hirschi 1990, p. 196). Anonymous stories posted on the website We Are All Criminals (www.weareallcriminals.org) contest that empirical claim.

CHAPTER SIX. BETTER LIVING IN STORY WORLDS

1. How we react to texts also depends on how we feel. That is, emotional states affect narrative experience (see Mar et al. 2011). Future research should explore how the *reciprocal* relation between narrative and emotion shapes social action.

2. Harm-doing without evident ill will—environmental degradation, for example—is a contemporary commonplace, which I grappled with in my analysis of the mood of satisfaction (chapter 5). But a benevolent kind of harm-doing, such as providing the wrong kind of aid to a struggling nation, may call for a slightly different approach. In these cases no one intends to harm, hence a less fraught identity project. Still, we might speculate that the benevolent harm-doer, ignorant of the actual needs of the recipient or the impacts of action or both, holds an attitude of indifference that my theory of narrative's emotional impact does address.

REFERENCES

Adams, Carol J. 1990. *The Sexual Politics of Meat: A Feminist-Vegetarian Critical Theory*. New York: Continuum.

Agnew, Robert. 1992. "Foundation for a General Strain Theory of Crime and Delinquency." *Criminology* 30 (1): 47–86.

Akers, Ronald L. 1991. "Self-Control as a General Theory of Crime." *Journal of Quantitative Criminology* 7 (2): 201–11.

———. 1998. *Social Learning and Social Structure: A General Theory of Crime and Deviance*. Boston: Northeastern University Press.

Alexander, Jeffrey C. 1992. "Citizen and Enemy as Symbolic Classification." In *Cultivating Differences: Symbolic Boundaries and the Making of Inequality*, edited by Michèle Lamont and Marcel Fournier, 289–308. Chicago: University of Chicago Press.

Alexander, Jeffrey, and Philip Smith. 2002. "The Strong Program in Cultural Theory: Elements of a Structural Hermeneutics." In *Handbook of Sociological Theory*, edited by Jonathan H. Turner, 135–50. New York: Kluwer.

Alexander, Michelle. 2012. *The New Jim Crow: Mass Incarceration in the Age of Colorblindness*. New York: New Press.

Althusser, Louis. 1971. *Lenin and Philosophy, and Other Essays*. London: New Left Books.

Altman, Rick. 2008. *A Theory of Narrative.* New York: Columbia University Press.

Alvarez, Alexander. 1997. "Adjusting to Genocide: The Techniques of Neutralization and the Holocaust." *Social Science History* 21 (2): 139–78.

Anderson, Elijah. 1999. *Code of the Street: Decency, Violence, and the Moral Life of the Inner City.* New York: W.W. Norton.

Andrews, Travis M. 2016. "Leading Philippine Presidential Contender: Gang Rape Victim 'So Beautiful' He Wishes He Had 'Been First.'" *Washington Post,* April 18. https://www.washingtonpost.com/news/morning-mix/wp/2016/04/18/leading-philippines-presidential-contender-gang-rape-victim-so-beautiful-he-wishes-he-had-been-first/?utm_term=.cd805106oof4.

Aquina, Karl, Americus Reed II, Stefan Thau, and Dan Freeman. 2007. "A Grotesque and Dark Beauty: How Moral Identity and Mechanisms of Moral Disengagement Influence Cognitive and Emotional Reactions to War." *Journal of Experimental Social Psychology* 43 (3): 385–92.

Arendt, Hannah. 1963. *Eichmann in Jerusalem: A Report on the Banality of Evil.* New York: Viking Press.

Aristotle. 1996. *Poetics.* Translated with an introduction and notes by Malcolm Heath. London: Penguin.

Austin, J. L. 1962. *How to Do Things with Words.* Cambridge, MA: Harvard University Press.

Auyoung, Elaine. 2013. "Partial Cues and Narrative Understanding in Anna Karenina." In *Stories and Minds: Cognitive Approaches to Literary Narratives,* edited by Lars Bernaerts, Dirk De Geest, Luc Herman, and Bart Vervaeck, 59–78. Lincoln: University of Nebraska Press.

Bamberg, Michael, and Alexandra Georgakopoulou. 2008. "Small Stories as a New Perspective in Narrative and Identity Analysis." *Text and Talk* 28 (3): 377–96.

Bandura, Albert. 1990. "Mechanisms of Moral Disengagement." In *Origins of Terrorism: Psychologies, Ideologies, Theologies, States of Mind,* edited by Walter Reich, 161–91. New York: Cambridge University Press.

———. 1999. "Moral Disengagement in the Perpetration of Inhumanities." *Personality and Social Psychology Review* 3 (3): 193–209.

Baroni, Raphaël. 2015. "Plots in Life and Fiction: A Cognitive Reconceptualization." *Književna Istorija (Literary History)* 47 (155): 41–56.

Barthes, Roland. 1957. *Mythologies.* Translated by Annette Lavers. Paris: Editions du Seuil.

———. 1977. "Introduction to the Structural Analysis of Narratives." In *Image, Music, Text,* 79–124. Translated by Stephen Heath. New York: Hill and Wang.

Baumeister, Roy F., Ellen Bratslavsky, Catrin Finkenauer, and Kathleen D. Vohs. 2001. "Bad Is Stronger Than Good." *Review of General Psychology* 5 (4): 323–70.

Becker, Ernest. 1973. *The Denial of Death.* New York: Free Press.

Bélanger-Vincent, Ariane. 2009. "Discourses That Make Torture Possible: The Abu Ghraib Case." *Explorations in Anthropology* 9 (1): 36–46.

Belknap, Robert L. 2016. *Plots.* New York: Columbia University Press.

Bem, Daryl J. 1972. "Self-Perception Theory." *Advances in Experimental Social Psychology* 6:1–62.

Benedek, Mathias, Roger Beaty, Emanuel Jauk, Karl Koschutnig, Andreas Fink, Paul J. Silvia, Beate Dunst, and Aljoscha C. Neubauer. 2014. "Creating Metaphors: The Neural Basis of Figurative Language Production." *NeuroImage* 90:99–106.

Beneke, Timothy. 1982. *Men on Rape.* New York: St. Martin's Press.

Berger, Peter L., and Thomas Luckmann. 1966. *The Social Construction of Reality: A Treatise in the Sociology of Knowledge.* New York: Anchor Books.

Berntzen, Lars Erik, and Sveinung Sandberg. 2014. "The Collective Nature of Lone Wolf Terrorism: Anders Behring Breivik and the Anti-Islamic Social Movement." *Terrorism and Political Violence* 26 (5): 759–79.

Bezdek, Matthew A., Richard J. Gerrig, William G. Wenzel, Jaemin Shin, Kate Pirog Revill, and Eric H. Schumacher. 2015. "Neural Evidence That Suspense Narrows Attentional Focus." *Neuroscience* 303:338–45.

Bonilla-Silva, Eduardo. 2017. *Racism without Racists: Color-Blind Racism and the Persistence of Racial Ideology in America.* 5th ed. Lanham, MD: Rowman and Littlefield.

Boruah, Bijoy H. 1988. *Fiction and Emotion: A Study in Aesthetics and the Philosophy of Mind.* Oxford: Clarendon Press.

Bourdieu, Pierre. 1977. *Outline of a Theory of Practice.* Translated by Richard Nice. Cambridge: Cambridge University Press.

Bourgois, Phillippe. 2003. *In Search of Respect: Selling Crack in El Barrio.* 2nd ed. Cambridge: Cambridge University Press.

Box, Steven. 1983. *Power, Crime, and Mystification.* New York: Tavistock.

Braithwaite, John. 1989. *Crime, Shame and Reintegration.* Cambridge: Cambridge University Press.

Brewer, William F., and Edward H. Lichenstein. 1982. "Stories Are to Entertain: A Structural-Affect Theory of Stories." *Journal of Pragmatics* 6 (5–6): 473–86.

Brockmeier, Jens. 2004. "What Makes a Story Coherent?" In *Communication and Metacommunication in Human Development*, edited by Angela Uchoa Branco and Jaan Valsiner, 285–306. Charlotte, NC: Information Age Publishing.

Brooks, Peter. 1984. *Reading for the Plot: Design and Intention in Narrative.* Cambridge, MA: Harvard University Press.

Bruner, Jerome. 1986. *Actual Minds, Possible Worlds.* Cambridge, MA: Harvard University Press.

Burke, Kenneth. 1945. *A Grammar of Motives.* Berkeley: University of California Press.

Burt, Martha R. 1980. "Cultural Myths and Supports for Rape." *Journal of Personality and Social Psychology* 38 (2): 217–30.

Busselle, Rick, and Helena Bilandzic. 2008. "Fictionality and Perceived Realism in Experiencing Stories: A Model of Narrative Comprehension and Engagement." *Communication Theory* 18 (2): 255–80.

Butler, Judith. 1990. *Gender Trouble: Feminism and the Subversion of Identity.* New York: Routledge.

Calhoun, Craig. 2001. "Putting Emotions in Their Place." In *Passionate Politics: Emotions and Social Movements*, edited by Goodwin, Jeff, James M. Jasper, and Francesca Polletta, 45–57. Chicago: University of Chicago Press.

Carruthers, Peter. 2002. "The Cognitive Functions of Language." *Behavioral and Brain Sciences* 25:657–726.

Chambers, Ross. 1984. *Story and Situation: Narrative Seduction and the Power of Fiction.* Minneapolis: University of Minnesota Press.

Citron, Francesca M.M., Jeremie Güsten, Nora Michaelis, and Adele E. Goldberg. 2016. "Conventional Metaphors in Longer Passages Evoke Affective Brain Response." *NeuroImage* 139:218–30.

Clandinin, D. Jean. 1992. "Narrative and Story in Teacher Education." In *Teachers and Teaching: From Classroom to Reflection*, edited by Tom Russell and Hugh Munby, 124–37. London: Falmer Press.

Clear, Todd R. 1994. *Harm in American Penology: Offenders, Victims, and Their Communities*. Albany: State University of New York Press.

Cohen, Albert K. 1955. *Delinquent Boys: The Culture of the Gang*. New York: Free Press.

Cohen, Jonathan. 2001. "Defining Identification: A Theoretical Look at the Identification of Audiences with Media Characters." *Mass Communication and Society* 4:245–64.

Cohen, Stanley. 2001. *States of Denial: Knowing about Atrocities and Suffering*. Cambridge, UK: Polity Press.

———. 2011. *Folk Devils and Moral Panics*. New York: Routledge.

Cohn, Carol. 1987. "Sex and Death in the Rational World of Defense Intellectuals." *Signs: Journal of Women in Culture and Society* 12 (4): 687–718.

Connell, R.W. 1995. *Masculinities: Knowledge, Power and Social Change*. Berkeley: University of California Press.

Cooper, Alexia, and Erica L. Smith. 2011. *Homicide Trends in the United States 1980–2008*. U.S. Department of Justice. https://www.bjs.gov/content/pub/pdf/htus8008.pdf.

Cordes, Bonnie. 2001. "When Terrorists Do the Talking: Reflections on Terrorist Literature." In *Inside Terrorist Organizations*, edited by David C. Rapoport, 150–71. 2nd ed. London: Frank Cass.

Culler, Jonathan. 2001. *The Pursuit of Signs: Semiotics, Literature, Deconstruction*. Ithaca, NY: Cornell University Press.

Currie, Gregory. 2010. *Narratives and Narrators: A Philosophy of Stories*. New York: Oxford University Press.

Dabiq. 2016. "Foreword." *The Murtadd Brotherhood*, 14. https://www.clarionproject.org/docs/Dabiq-Issue-14.pdf.

Davis, Joseph E. 2002. "Narrative and Social Movements: The Power of Stories." In *Stories of Change: Narrative and Social Movements*, edited by Joseph E. Davis, 3–29. Albany: State University of New York Press.

Davis, Lydia. 1986. *Break It Down: Stories.* New York: Farrar, Straus and Giroux.

De Fina, Anna, and Alexandra Georgakopoulou. 2012. *Analyzing Narrative Discourse and Sociolinguistic Perspectives.* Cambridge: Cambridge University Press.

Douglas-Gabriel, Danielle, and Tracy Jan. 2017. "DeVos Called HBCUs 'Pioneers' of 'School Choice.' It Didn't Go Over Well." *Washington Post,* February 28. https://www.washingtonpost.com/news/grade-point/wp/2017/02/28/devos-called-hbcus-pioneers-of-school-choice-it-didnt-go-over-well/?utm_term=aa7820a19550.

Eagleton, Terry. 1991. *Ideology: An Introduction.* London: Verso.

Eakin, Paul John. 2006. "Narrative Identity and Narrative Imperialism: A Response to Galen Strawson and James Phelan." *Narrative* 14 (2): 180–87.

Edgerton, Franklin. 1936. "Indirect Suggestion in Poetry: A Hindu Theory of Literary Aesthetics." *Proceedings of the American Philosophical Society* 76 (5): 687–706.

Ekman, Paul. 1984. "Expression and the Nature of Emotion." In *Approaches to Emotion,* edited by Klaus R. Scherer and Paul Ekman, 319–43. Hillsdale, NJ: Lawrence Erlbaum.

———. 1992. "An Argument for Basic Emotions." *Cognition and Emotion* 6 (3/4): 169–200.

———. 1999. "Basic Emotions." In *The Handbook of Cognition and Emotion,* edited by T. Dalgleish and T. Power, 45–60. Sussex, UK: John Wiley and Sons.

Elias, Norbert. 2000. *The Civilizing Process: Sociogenetic and Psychogenetic Investigations.* Rev. ed. Malden, MA: Blackwell.

Ellis, Albert. 1973. *Humanistic Psychotherapy.* Secaucus, NJ: Lyle Stuart.

Ewick, Patricia, and Susan S. Silbey. 1995. "Subversive Stories and Hegemonic Tales: Toward a Sociology of Narrative." *Law and Society Review* 29 (2): 197–226.

Ezzy, Douglas. 2000. "Illness Narratives: Time, Hope and HIV." *Social Science and Medicine* 50 (5): 605–17.

Fainsilber, Lynn, and Andrew Ortony. 1987. "Metaphorical Uses of Language in the Expression of Emotions." *Metaphor and Symbolic Activity* 2 (4): 239–50.

Faludi, Susan. 1999. *Stiffed: The Betrayal of the American Man.* New York: HarperCollins.

Fantasia, Rick, and Eric L. Hirsch. 2003. "Culture in Rebellion: The Appropriation and Transformation of the Veil in the Algerian Revolution." In *Social Movements and Culture*, edited by Hank Johnston and Bert Klandermans, 144–59. London: Routledge.

Feeley, Malcolm M., and Jonathan Simon. 1992. "The New Penology: Notes on the Emerging Strategy of Corrections and Its Implications." *Criminology* 30:449–74.

Fehr, Beverley, and James A. Russell. 1984. "Concept of Emotion Viewed from a Prototype Perspective." *Journal of Experimental Psychology: General* 113 (3): 464–86.

Feild, Hubert S. 1978. "Attitudes toward Rape: A Comparative Analysis of Police, Rapists, Crisis Counselors, and Citizens." *Journal of Personality and Social Psychology* 36 (2): 156–79.

Feldman, Allen. 1991. *Formations of Violence: The Narrative of the Body and Political Terror in Northern Ireland.* Chicago: University of Chicago Press.

Ferrell, Jeff, Keith Hayward, Wayne Morrison, and Mike Presdee, eds. 2004. *Cultural Criminology Unleashed.* London: Glasshouse Press.

Fine, Gary Alan. 2002. "The Storied Group: Social Movements as 'Bundles of Narratives.'" In *Stories of Change: Narrative and Social Movements*, edited by Joseph E. Davis, 229–45. Albany: State University of New York Press.

Fisher, Walter R. 1987. *Human Communication as Narration: Toward a Philosophy of Reason, Value, and Action.* Columbia: University of South Carolina Press.

Fleetwood, Jennifer. 2016. "Narrative Habitus: Thinking through Structure/Agency in the Narratives of Offenders." *Crime, Media, Culture* 12 (2): 173–92.

Forster, E. M. 1927. *Aspects of the Novel.* New York: Harcourt, Brace.

Foucault, Michel. 2000. "Truth and Power." In *Essential Works of Foucault 1954–1984*, edited by J.B. Faubion, 111–33. New York: New Press.

Fox, James A., and Jack Levin. 1998. "Multiple Homicide: Patterns of Serial and Mass Murder." *Crime and Justice: A Review of Research* 23:407–55.

Frank, Arthur W. 2010a. *Letting Stories Breathe: A Socio-narratology.* Chicago: University of Chicago Press.

———. 2010b. "In Defence of Narrative Exceptionalism." *Sociology of Health and Illness* 32 (4): 665–67.

Frankl, Viktor E. 1984. *Man's Search for Meaning: An Introduction to Logotherapy.* 3rd ed. New York: Touchstone.

Freytag, Gustav. 1895. *Technique of the Drama: An Exposition of Dramatic Composition and Art.* Chicago: S.C. Griggs.

Frijda, Nico H. 1988. "The Laws of Emotion." *American Psychologist* 43 (5): 349–58.

Frye, Northrop. 1957. *Anatomy of Criticism: Four Essays.* Princeton, NJ: Princeton University Press.

Fuchs, Erin. 2015. "It's Incredible How Much Safer America Has Become since the 1980s." *Business Insider*, January 27. http://www.businessinsider.com/fbi-crime-report-shows-america-is-still-getting-safer-2015-1.

Gabriel, Trip. 2016. "Trump Sliding? Die-Hard Fans Refuse to Buy It." *New York Times*, October 12. http://www.nytimes.com/2016/10/12/us/politics/donald-trump-voters.html?_r=0.

Gadd, David, and Tony Jefferson. 2007. *Psychosocial Criminology: An Introduction.* London: Sage.

Gamson, William A. 1988. "Political Discourse and Collective Action." *International Social Movement Research* 1:219–44.

———. 1992. *Talking Politics.* Cambridge: Cambridge University Press.

———. 1995. "Constructing Social Protest." In *Social Movements and Culture*, edited by Hank Johnston and Bert Klandermans, 85–106. Minneapolis: University of Minnesota Press.

Gamson, William A., Bruce Fireman, and Steven Rytina. 1982. *Encounters with Unjust Authority.* Homewood, IL: Dorsey Press.

Garfinkel, Harold. 1967. "What Is Ethnomethodology?" In *Studies in Ethnomethodology*, edited by Harold Garfinkel, 1–34. Englewood Cliffs, NJ: Prentice-Hall.

Geis, Gilbert. 2000. "On the Absence of Self-Control as the Basis for a General Theory of Crime: A Critique." *Theoretical Criminology* 4 (1): 35–53.

Gerrig, Richard J. 1993. *Experiencing Narrative Worlds: On the Psychological Activities of Reading.* New Haven, CT: Yale University Press.

Gibbs, Raymond W., Jr. 1994. *The Poetics of Mind: Figurative Thought, Language, and Understanding.* Cambridge: Cambridge University Press.

Gibbs, Raymond W., Jr., John S. Leggitt, and Elizabeth A. Turner. 2002. "What's Special about Figurative Language in Emotional Communication?" In *The Verbal Communication of Emotions: Interdisciplinary Perspectives*, edited by Susan R. Fussell, 125–49. London: Routledge.

Gilligan, Carol. 1982. *In a Different Voice: Psychological Theory and Women's Development.* Cambridge, MA: Harvard University Press.

Glucksberg, Sam. 2001. *Understanding Figurative Language: From Metaphors to Idioms.* New York: Oxford University Press.

Goffman, Erving. 1959. *The Presentation of Self in Everyday Life.* New York: Anchor Books.

———. 1974. *Frame Analysis: An Essay on the Organization of Experience.* New York: Harper & Row.

Goldhagen, Daniel Jonah. 1996. *Hitler's Willing Executioners: Ordinary Germans and the Holocaust.* New York: Vintage.

Goldstein, Matthew, and Stacy Cowley. 2017. "Casting Wall Street as Victim, Trump Leads Charge on Deregulation." *New York Times*, November 28. https://www.nytimes.com/2017/11/27/business/financial-regulation-rollback-trump.html

Goodwin, Jeff, James M. Jasper, and Francesca Polletta. 2001. "Introduction: Why Emotions Matter." In *Passionate Politics: Emotions and Social Movements*, edited by Jeff Goodwin, James M. Jasper, and Francesca Polletta, 1–24. Chicago: University of Chicago Press.

Gordon, Avery F. 1997. *Ghostly Matters: Haunting and the Sociological Imagination.* Minneapolis: University of Minnesota Press.

Gottfredson, Michael R., and Travis Hirschi. 1990. *A General Theory of Crime.* Stanford, CA: Stanford University Press.

Gottschall, Jonathan. 2012. *The Storytelling Animal: How Stories Make Us Human.* Boston: Houghton Mifflin Harcourt.

Graesser, Arthur C., Brent Olde, and Bianca Klettke. 2002. "How Does the Mind Construct and Represent Stories?" In *Narrative Impact: Social and Cognitive Foundations*, edited by Melanie C. Green, Jeffrey J. Strange, and Timothy C. Brock, 229–62. Mahwah, NJ: Lawrence Erlbaum.

Graesser, Arthur C., Murray Singer, and Tom Trabasso. 1994. "Constructing Inferences during Narrative Text Comprehension." *Psychological Review* 101 (3): 371–95.

Gray, Herman. 2013. "Subject(ed) to Recognition." *American Quarterly* 65 (4): 771–98.

Green, Melanie C., and Timothy C. Brock. 2000. "The Role of Transportation in the Persuasiveness of Public Narratives." *Journal of Personality and Social Psychology* 79 (5): 701–21.

———. 2002. "In the Mind's Eye: Transportation-Imagery Model of Narrative Persuasion." In *Narrative Impact: Social and Cognitive Foundations*, edited by Melanie C. Green, Jeffrey J. Strange, and Timothy C. Brock, 315–41. Mahwah, NJ: Lawrence Erlbaum.

Green, Melanie C., Jennifer Garst, and Timothy C. Brock. 2004. "The Power of Fiction: Determinants and Boundaries." In *The Psychology of Entertainment Media: Blurring the Lines between Entertainment and Persuasion*, edited by L.J. Shrum, 161–76. Mahwah, NJ: Lawrence Erlbaum.

Grossman, Michele. 2015. "Disenchantments: Counter-terror Narratives and Conviviality." In *Cultural, Religious and Political Contestations: The Multicultural Challenge*, edited by Fethi Mansouri, 71–89. Cham, Switzerland: Springer International Publishing Switzerland.

Hagan, John, and Wenona Rymond-Richmond. 2008. "The Collective Dynamics of Racial Dehumanization and Genocidal Victimization in Darfur." *American Sociological Review* 73:875–902.

———. 2009. *Darfur and the Crime of Genocide.* New York: Cambridge University Press.

Halverson, Jeffry R., H.L. Goodall Jr., and Steven R. Corman. 2011. *Master Narratives of Islamist Extremism.* New York: Palgrave Macmillan.

Hanne, Michael. 1994. *The Power of the Story: Fiction and Political Change.* Providence, RI: Berghahn Books.

Harcourt, Bernard E. 2001. *Illusion of Order: The False Promise of Broken Windows Policing.* Cambridge, MA: Harvard University Press.

Harold, James. 2005. "Infected by Evil." *Philosophical Explorations* 8 (2): 173–87.

Haslam, Nick. 2006. "Dehumanization: An Integrative Review." *Personality and Social Psychology Review* 10 (3): 252–64.

Hatzfeld, Jean. 2003. *Machete Season: The Killers in Rwanda Speak.* New York: Picador.

Herman, David. 2002. *Story Logic: Problems and Possibilities of Narrative.* Lincoln, NE: University of Nebraska Press.

———. 2009. *Basic Elements of Narrative.* Malden, MA: Wiley-Blackwell.

Herman, Luc, and Bart Vervaeck. 2009. "Narrative Interest as Cultural Negotiation." *Narrative* 17 (1): 111–29.

Herrnstein Smith, Barbara. 1980. "Narrative Versions, Narrative Theories." *Critical Inquiry* 7 (1): 213–36.

Hinton, Alexander Laban. 1996. "Agents of Death: Explaining the Cambodian Genocide in Terms of Psychosocial Dissonance." *American Anthropologist* 98 (4): 818–31.

Hirschi, Travis. 1969. *Causes of Delinquency.* Berkeley: University of California Press.

Hirschi, Travis, and Michael Gottfredson. 1983. "Age and the Explanation of Crime." *American Journal of Sociology* 89 (3): 552–84.

———. 2000. "In Defense of Self-Control." *Theoretical Criminology* 4 (1): 55–69.

Hochschild, Arlie Russell. 2016. *Strangers in Their Own Land: Anger and Mourning on the American Right.* New York: New Press.

Hodge, Robert, and Gunther Kress. 1993. *Language as Ideology.* 2nd ed. London: Routledge.

Hoffman, Bruce, and Thomas M. Vander Ven. 2007. "Mother Blame and Delinquency Claims: Juvenile Delinquency and Maternal

Responsibility." In *Youth Violence and Delinquency: Monsters and Myths*, edited by Marilyn D. McShane and Franklin P. Williams III, 1:159–75. Westport, CT: Praeger.

Hogan, Patrick Colm. 2003. *The Mind and Its Stories: Narrative Universals and Human Emotions.* Cambridge: Cambridge University Press.

———. 2006. "Narrative Universals, Nationalism, and Sacrificial Terror: From Nosferatu to Nazism." *Film Studies* 8 (1): 93–105.

Hollway, Wendy, and Tony Jefferson. 2000. *Doing Qualitative Research Differently: Free Association, Narrative and the Interview Method.* London: Sage.

Howard, Judith A. 1995. "Social Cognition." In *Sociological Perspectives on Social Psychology*, edited by Karen S. Cook, Gary Alan Fine, and James S. House, 90–117. Boston: Allyn and Bacon.

Huggins, Martha K., Mika Haritos-Fatouros, and Philip G. Zimbardo. 2002. *Violence Workers: Police Torturers and Murderers Reconstruct Brazilian Atrocities.* Berkeley: University of California Press.

Hughes, Everett C. 1964. "Good People and Dirty Work." In *The Other Side: Perspectives on Deviance*, edited by Howard S. Becker, 23–36. New York: Free Press.

Hyvärinen, Matti. 2008. "'Life as Narrative' Revisited." *Partial Answers* 6/2:261–77.

Iser, Wolfgang. 1972. "The Reading Process: A Phenomenological Approach." *New Literary History* 3 (2): 279–99.

———. 1978. *The Act of Reading: A Theory of Aesthetic Response.* Baltimore: Johns Hopkins University Press.

Jackson-Jacobs, Curtis. 2004. "Taking a Beating: The Narrative Gratifications of Fighting as an Underdog." In *Cultural Criminology Unleashed*, edited by Jeff Ferrell, Keith Hayward, Wayne Morrison, and Mike Presdee, 231–44. London: Glasshouse Press.

Jacobs, Arthur M. 2015. "Towards a Neurocognitive Poetics Model of Literary Reading." In *Cognitive Neuroscience of Natural Language Use*, edited by Roel M. Willems, 135–59. Cambridge: Cambridge University Press.

Jacobs, Ronald N. 2002. "The Narrative Integration of Personal and Collective Identity in Social Movements." In *Narrative Impact: Social and*

Cognitive Foundations, edited by Melanie C. Green, Jeffrey J. Strange, and Timothy C. Brock, 205–28. Mahwah, NJ: Lawrence Erlbaum.

Jasper, James. 1998. "The Emotions of Protest: Affective and Reactive Emotions in and around Social Movements." *Sociological Forum* 13 (3): 397–424.

Jenkins, Richard. 2004. *Social Identity*. 2nd ed. London: Routledge.

Johnson, Devon. 2009. "Anger about Crime and Support for Punitive Criminal Justice Policies." *Punishment & Society* 11 (1): 51–66.

Johnson-Laird, P. N., and Keith Oatley. 1989. "The Language of Emotions: An Analysis of a Semantic Field." *Cognition and Emotion* 3 (2): 81–123.

Joosse, Paul, Sandra M. Bucerius, and Sara K. Thompson. 2015. "Narratives and Counternarratives: Somali Canadians on Recruitment as Foreign Fighters to Al-Shabaab." *British Journal of Criminology* 55:811–32.

Kang, Cecilia, and Adam Goldman. 2016. "In Washington Pizzeria Attack, Fake News Brought Real Guns." *New York Times*, December 5. http://www.nytimes.com/2016/12/05/business/media/comet-ping-pong-pizza-shooting-fake-news-consequences.html.

Katz, Jack. 1988. *Seductions of Crime: The Moral and Sensual Attractions of Doing Evil*. New York: Basic Books.

———. 1999. *How Emotions Work*. Chicago: University of Chicago Press.

Keen, Suzanne. 2007. *Empathy and the Novel*. New York: Oxford University Press.

Keeton, Robert M. 2015. "'The Race of Pale Men Should Increase and Multiply': Religious Narratives and Indian Removal." In *Narrative Criminology: Understanding Stories of Crime*, edited by Lois Presser and Sveinung Sandberg, 125–49. New York and London: New York University Press.

Kelling, George L., and Catherine M. Coles. 1996. *Fixing Broken Windows: Restoring Order and Reducing Crime in Our Communities*. New York: Simon and Schuster.

Kelman, Herbert C. 1973. "Violence without Moral Restraint: Reflections on the Dehumanization of Victims and Victimizers." *Journal of Social Issues* 29 (4): 25–61.

Kemper, Theodore D. 1984. "Power, Status, and Emotions: A Sociological Contribution to a Psychophysiological Domain." In *Approaches to Emotion*, edited by Klaus R. Scherer and Paul Ekman, 369–96. Hillsdale, NJ: Lawrence Erlbaum.

Kendi, Ibram X. 2017. "Racial Progress Is Real. But So Is Racist Progress." *New York Times*, January 21. https://www.nytimes.com/2017/01/21/opinion/sunday/racial-progress-is-real-but-so-is-racist-progress.html?action=click&pgtype=Homepage&clickSource=story-heading&module=opinion-c-col-left-region®ion=opinion-c-col-left-region&WT.nav=opinion-c-col-left-region&_r=0.

Kepel, Gilles, and Jean-Pierre Milelli, eds. 2008. *Al Qaeda in Its Own Words*. Cambridge, MA: Belknap Press of Harvard University Press.

Kerby, Anthony Paul. 1991. *Narrative and the Self*. Bloomington: Indiana University Press.

Kermode, Frank. 1967. *The Sense of an Ending: Studies in the Theory of Fiction*. New York: Oxford University Press.

Klemperer, Victor. 2007. *The Language of the Third Reich: LTI—Lingua Tertii Imperii: A Philologist's Notebook*. Translated by Martin Brady. London: Continuum.

Knoxnews.com. 2009. "Church Shooter Pleads Guilty; Letter Released." *Knoxville News-Sentinel*, February 10. http://archive.knoxnews.com/news/local/church-shooter-pleads-guilty-letter-released-ep-410394311-359596061.html.

Kurtz, Don L., and Lindsey Upton. 2017. "War Stories and Occupying Soldiers: A Narrative Approach to Understanding Police Culture and Community Conflict." *Critical Criminology* 25 (4): 539–58.

Labov, William. 1972. "The Transformation of Experience in Narrative Syntax." In *Language in the Inner City: Studies in the Black English Vernacular*, 354–96. Philadelphia: University of Pennsylvania Press.

Labov, William, and Joshua Waletzky. 1967. "Narrative Analysis: Oral Versions of Personal Experience." In *Essays on the Verbal and Visual Arts*, edited by June Helm, 12–44. Seattle: University of Washington Press.

Lai, Kiam Loong Daniel. 2015. "Constructing Victimhood: Opposition to Legislation Protecting LGBT Students against Bullying." PhD diss., University of Tennessee.

Lakoff, George. 2002. *Moral Politics: How Liberals and Conservatives Think.* 2nd ed. Chicago: University of Chicago Press.

Lakoff, George, and Mark Johnson. 1980. *Metaphors We Live By.* Chicago: University of Chicago Press.

Lamont, Michèle, and Virág Molnár. 2002. "The Study of Boundaries in the Social Sciences." *Annual Review of Sociology* 28:167–95.

Lang, Peter J. 1994. "The Varieties of Emotional Experience: A Meditation on James-Lange Theory." *Psychological Review* 101 (2): 211–21.

Lazarus, Richard S. 1991. *Emotion and Adaptation.* New York: Oxford University Press.

Le Bon, Gustave. 1903. *The Crowd: A Study of the Popular Mind.* London: T. Fisher Unwin.

Lévi-Strauss, Claude. 1966. *The Savage Mind.* Chicago: University of Chicago Press.

Lieberman, Ben. 2006. "Nationalist Narratives, Violence between Neighbours and Ethnic Cleansing in Bosnia-Hercegovina: A Case of Cognitive Dissonance?" *Journal of Genocide Research* 8 (3): 295–309.

Linde, Charlotte. 1993. *Life Stories: Creation of Coherence.* New York: Oxford University Press.

———. 2000. "The Acquisition of a Speaker by a Story: How History Becomes Memory and Identity." *Ethos* 28 (4): 608–32.

Lombroso, Cesare. 1876. *L'uomo delinquente.* Milan: Hoepli.

Loseke, Donileen R. 2003. *Thinking about Social Problems: An Introduction to Constructionist Perspectives.* 2nd ed. New York: Aldine de Gruyter.

Lyons-Padilla, Sarah, Michele J. Gelfand, Hedieh Mirahmadi, Mehreen Farooq, and Marieke van Egmond. 2015. "Belonging Nowhere: Marginalization and Radicalization Risk among Muslim Immigrants." *Behavioral Science and Policy* 1 (2): 1–12.

Lyotard, Jean-François. 1984. *The Postmodern Condition: A Report on Knowledge.* Minneapolis: University of Minnesota Press.

Maan, Ajit. 2015. *Counter-terrorism: Narrative Strategies.* Lanham, MD: University Press of America.

MacIntyre, Alasdair. 1981. *After Virtue.* Notre Dame, IN: University of Notre Dame Press.

Maier-Katkin, Daniel, Daniel P. Mears, and Thomas J. Bernard. 2009. "Towards a Criminology of Crimes against Humanity." *Theoretical Criminology* 13 (2): 227–55.

Maikovich, Andrea Kohn. 2005. "A New Understanding of Terrorism Using Cognitive Dissonance Principles." *Journal for the Theory of Social Behaviour* 35 (4): 373–97.

Manji, Rahim, Lois Presser, and Leigh T. Dickey. 2014. "Passivity, Harm, and Injustice." *Contemporary Justice Review* 17 (1): 47–62.

Mar, Raymond A. 2004. "The Neuropsychology of Narrative: Story Comprehension, Story Production and Their Interrelation." *Neuropsychologia* 42 (10): 1414–34.

Mar, Raymond A., and Keith Oatley. 2008. "The Function of Fiction Is the Abstraction and Simulation of Social Experience." *Perspectives on Psychological Science* 3 (3): 173–92.

Mar, Raymond A., Keith Oatley, Maja Djikic, and Justin Mullin. 2011. "Emotion and Narrative Fiction: Interactive Influences before, during, and after Reading." *Cognition and Emotion* 25 (5): 818–33.

Mason, Carol. 2002. *Killing for Life: The Apocalyptic Narrative of Pro-life Politics.* Ithaca, NY: Cornell University Press.

Massumi, Brian. 2010. "The Future Birth of the Affective Fact: The Political Ontology of Threat." In *The Affect Theory Reader*, edited by Melissa Gregg and Gregory J. Seigworth, 52–70. Durham, NC: Duke University Press.

Matravers, Derek. 1991. "Art and the Feelings and Emotions." *British Journal of Aesthetics* 31 (4): 322–31.

Matza, David. 1964. *Delinquency and Drift.* New York: Wiley.

McAdams, Dan P. 1999. "Personal Narratives and the Life Story." In *Handbook of Personality: Theory and Research*, edited by Lawrence A. Pervin and Oliver P. John, 478–500. 2nd ed. New York: Guilford.

McDonnell, Terence E., Christopher A. Bail, and Iddo Tavory. 2017. "A Theory of Resonance." *Sociological Theory* 35 (1): 1–14.

McLaughlin, Neil. 2014. "Escapes from Freedom: Political Extremism, Conspiracy Theories, and the Sociology of Emotions." In *The Unhappy Divorce of Sociology and Psychoanalysis*, edited by Lynn Chancer and John Andrews, 161–89. London: Palgrave Macmillan.

Merton, Robert K. 1938. "Social Structure and Anomie." *American Sociological Review* 3:672–82.

Messerschmidt, James W. 1997. *Crime as Structured Action: Gender, Race, Class, and Crime in the Making.* Thousand Oaks, CA: Sage.

———. 2000. *Nine Lives: Adolescent Masculinities, the Body, and Violence.* Boulder, CO: Westview Press.

Messner, Steven F., and Richard Rosenfeld. 1994. *Crime and the American Dream.* Belmont, CA: Wadsworth.

Miller, Walter B. 1958. "Lower Class Culture as a Generating Milieu of Gang Delinquency." *Journal of Social Issues* 14 (3): 5–19.

Mink, Louis O. 1970. "History and Fiction as Modes of Comprehension." *New Literary History* 1 (3): 541–58.

Minow, Martha. 2002. *Breaking the Cycles of Hatred: Memory, Law, and Repair.* Princeton, NJ: Princeton University Press.

Moran, Rachel. 2015. *Paid For: My Journey through Prostitution.* New York: W. W. Norton.

Nabi, Robin L., and Melanie Green. 2015. "The Role of a Narrative's Emotional Flow in Promoting Persuasive Outcomes." *Media Psychology* 18:137–62.

Nell, Victor. 1988. *Lost in a Book: The Psychology of Reading for Pleasure.* New Haven, CT: Yale University Press.

———. 2002. "Mythic Structures in Narrative: The Domestication of Immortality." In *Narrative Impact: Social and Cognitive Foundations,* edited by Melanie C. Green, Jeffrey J. Strange, and Timothy C. Brock, 17–37. Mahwah, NJ: Lawrence Erlbaum.

Nussbaum, Martha C. 2001. *Upheavals of Thought: The Intelligence of Emotions.* Cambridge: Cambridge University Press.

Oatley, Keith. 1992. *Best Laid Schemes: The Psychology of Emotions.* Cambridge: Cambridge University Press.

———. 1999. "Why Fiction May Be Twice as True as Fact: Fiction as Cognitive and Emotional Simulation." *Review of General Psychology* 3 (2): 101–17.

———. 2002. "Emotions and the Story Worlds of Fiction." In *Narrative Impact: Social and Cognitive Foundations,* edited by Melanie C. Green, Jeffrey J. Strange, and Timothy C. Brock, 39–69. Mahwah, NJ: Lawrence Erlbaum.

Oatley, Keith, and P.N. Johnson-Laird. 1987. "Towards a Cognitive Theory of Emotions." *Cognition and Emotion* 1 (1): 29–50.

Obermann, Marie-Louise. 2011. "Moral Disengagement among Bystanders to School Bullying." *Journal of School Violence* 10 (3): 239–57.

Oberschall, Anthony. 2000. "The Manipulation of Ethnicity: From Ethnic Cooperation to Violence and War in Yugoslavia." *Ethnic and Racial Studies* 23 (6): 982–1001.

Opotow, Susan. 1993. "Animals and the Scope of Justice." *Journal of Social Issues* 49 (1): 71–85.

Ortony, Andrew. 1975. "Why Metaphors Are Necessary and Not Just Nice." *Educational Theory* 25:45–53.

Ortony, Andrew, Gerald L. Clore, and Allan Collins. 1988. *The Cognitive Structure of Emotions.* New York: Cambridge University Press.

Orwell, George. 1968. "Politics and the English Language." In *The Collected Essays, Journalism and Letters of George Orwell.* Vol. 4, *In Front of Your Nose, 1945–1950*, edited by Sonia Orwell and Ian Angus, 127–40. New York: Harcourt, Brace, Jovanovich.

Petitta, Laura, Tahira M. Probst, and Claudio Barbaranelli. 2015. "Safety Culture, Moral Disengagement, and Accident Underreporting." *Journal of Business Ethics* 141 (3): 1–16.

Phelan, James. 1989. *Reading People, Reading Plots: Character, Progression, and the Interpretation of Narrative.* Chicago: University of Chicago Press.

———. 2005. "Who's Here? Thoughts on Narrative Identity and Narrative Imperialism." *Narrative* 13:205–10.

Polanyi, Livia. 1985. *Telling the American Story: A Structural and Cultural Analysis of Conversational Storytelling.* Norwood, NJ: Ablex.

Polichak, James W., and Richard J. Gerrig. 2002. "'Get Up and Win!' Participatory Responses to Narrative." In *Narrative Impact: Social and Cognitive Foundations*, edited by Melanie C. Green, Jeffrey J. Strange, and Timothy C. Brock, 71–95. Mahwah, NJ: Lawrence Erlbaum.

Polletta, Francesca. 2006. *It Was Like a Fever: Storytelling in Protest and Politics.* Chicago: University of Chicago Press.

Polonoff, David. 1987. "Self-Deception." *Social Research* 54 (1): 45–53.

Pratt, Travis C., and Francis T. Cullen. 2000. "The Empirical Status of Gottfredson and Hirschi's General Theory of Crime: A Meta-analysis." *Criminology* 38 (3): 931–64.

Presdee, Mike. 2000. *Cultural Criminology and the Carnival of Crime*. London: Routledge.

Presser, Lois. 2004. "Violent Offenders, Moral Selves: Constructing Identities and Accounts in the Research Interview." *Social Problems* 51 (1): 82–101.

———. 2005. "Negotiating Power and Narrative in Research: Implications for Feminist Methodology." *Signs: Journal of Women in Culture and Society* 30 (4): 2067–90.

———. 2008. *Been a Heavy Life: Stories of Violent Men*. Urbana: University of Illinois Press.

———. 2009. "The Narratives of Offenders." *Theoretical Criminology* 13 (2): 177–200.

———. 2012. "Getting on Top through Mass Murder: Narrative, Metaphor, and Violence." *Crime, Media, Culture* 8 (1): 3–21.

———. 2013. *Why We Harm*. New Brunswick, NJ: Rutgers University Press.

———. 2016. "Criminology and the Narrative Turn." *Crime, Media, Culture* 12 (2): 137–51.

Presser, Lois, and Sveinung Sandberg, eds. 2015. *Narrative Criminology: Understanding Stories of Crime*. New York and London: New York University Press.

Prince, Gerald. 1992. *Narrative as Theme: Studies in French Fiction*. Lincoln: University of Nebraska Press.

Propp, Vladimir. 1968. *Morphology of the Folktale*. Translated by Laurence Scott. Austin: University of Texas Press.

Quinney, Richard. 1970. *The Social Reality of Crime*. Boston: Little, Brown.

Ricoeur, Paul. 1984. *Time and Narrative*. Vol. 1. Translated by Kathleen McLaughlin and David Pellauer. Chicago: University of Chicago Press.

Riessman, Catherine Kohler. 1993. *Narrative Analysis*. Newbury Park, CA: Sage.

Roberts, Julian V., and Michael J. Hough. 2005. *Understanding Public Attitudes to Criminal Justice*. Maidenhead, Berkshire: Open University Press.

Rojo, Ana, Marina Ramos, and Javier Valenzuela. 2014. "The Emotional Impact of Translation: A Heart Rate Study." *Journal of Pragmatics* 71:31–44.

Rondón, Andrés Miguel. 2017. "In Venezuela We Couldn't Stop Chávez. Don't Make the Same Mistakes We Did." *Washington Post*, January 27. https://www.washingtonpost.com/posteverything/wp/2017/01/27/in-venezuela-we-couldnt-stop-chavez-dont-make-the-same-mistakes-we-did/?utm_term=.a22af77b617f&wpisrc=nl_most-draw14&wpmm=1.

Rosenwald, George C., and Richard L. Ochberg. 1992. "Introduction: Life Stories, Cultural Politics, and Self-Understanding." In *Storied Lives: The Cultural Politics of Self-Understanding*, edited by George C. Rosenwald and Richard L. Ochberg, 1–18. New Haven, CT: Yale University Press.

Sandberg, Sveinung. 2013. "Are Self-Narratives Strategic or Determined, Unified or Fragmented? Reading Breivik's Manifesto in Light of Narrative Criminology." *Acta Sociologica* 56 (1): 69–83.

———. 2016. "The Importance of Stories Untold: Life-Story, Event-Story, and Trope." *Crime, Media, Culture* 12 (2): 153–71.

Sandberg, Sveinung, Sébastien Tutenges, and Heith Copes. 2015. "Stories of Violence: A Narrative Criminological Study of Ambiguity." *British Journal of Criminology* 55 (6): 1168–86.

Sanders, Meghan S., and Mina Tsay-Vogel. 2016. "Beyond Heroes and Villains: Examining Explanatory Mechanisms Underlying Moral Disengagement." *Mass Communication and Society* 19:230–52.

Sarbin, Theodore R., ed. 1986. *Narrative Psychology: The Storied Nature of Human Conduct*. New York: Praeger.

Sartre, Jean-Paul. 1948. *The Emotions: Outline of a Theory*. New York: Philosophical Library.

Sauter, Disa A., Frank Eisner, Paul Ekman, and Sophie K. Scott. 2010. "Cross-Cultural Recognition of Basic Emotions through Nonverbal Emotional Vocalizations." *Proceedings of the National Academy of Sciences of the United States of America* 107 (6): 2408–12.

Savelsberg, Joachim J. 2010. *Crime and Human Rights.* Los Angeles: Sage.

Savelsberg, Joachim, J., and Ryan D. King. 2011. *American Memories: Atrocities and the Law.* New York: Russell Sage Foundation.

Schank, Roger C., and Robert P. Abelson. 1995. "Knowledge and Memory: The Real Story." In *Advances in Social Cognition* VIII, edited by Robert S. Wyer Jr., 1–86. Hillsdale, NJ: Lawrence Erlbaum.

Schank, Roger C., and Tamara R. Berman. 2002. "The Pervasive Role of Stories in Knowledge and Action." In *Narrative Impact: Social and Cognitive Foundations*, edited by Melanie C. Green, Jeffrey J. Strange, and Timothy C. Brock, 287–313. Mahwah, NJ: Lawrence Erlbaum.

Schechtman, Marya. 1997. *The Constitution of Selves.* Ithaca, NY: Cornell University Press.

———. 2007. "Stories, Lives, and Basic Survival: A Refinement and Defense of the Narrative View." *Royal Institute of Philosophy Supplement* 60:155–78.

Scheff, Thomas J. 1994. *Bloody Revenge: Emotions, Nationalism, and War.* Boulder, CO: Westview Press.

Schept, Judah. 2015. *Progressive Punishment: Job Loss, Jail Growth, and the Neoliberal Logic of Carceral Expansion.* New York and London: New York University Press.

Schiffrin, Deborah. 1996. "Narrative as Self-Portrait: Sociolinguistic Constructions of Identity." *Language in Society* 25 (2): 167–203.

Schwendinger, Julia R., and Herman Schwendinger. 1974. "Rape Myths: In Legal, Theoretical, and Everyday Practice." *Crime and Social Justice* 1:18–26.

Scott, Marvin B., and Stanford M. Lyman. 1968. "Accounts." *American Sociological Review* 33 (1): 46–62.

Sharpe, Christina. 2016. *In the Wake: On Blackness and Being.* Durham, NC: Duke University Press.

Shaw, Clifford, and Henry D. McKay. 1942. *Juvenile Delinquency and Urban Areas.* Chicago: University of Chicago Press.

Silbert, Lauren J., Christopher J. Honey, Erez Simony, David Poeppel, and Uri Hasson. 2014. "Coupled Neural Systems Underlie the Production and Comprehension of Naturalistic Narrative Speech." *Proceedings of the National Academy of Sciences* 111 (43): E4687–E4696.

Smith, Dorothy E. 1987. *The Everyday World as Problematic.* Boston: Northeastern University Press.

Smith, Megan K., Robert Trivers, and William von Hippel. 2017. "Self-Deception Facilitates Interpersonal Persuasion." *Journal of Economic Psychology* 63:93–101. http://www.sciencedirect.com/science/article/pii/S0167487016301854#.

Smith, N. Kyle, John T. Cacioppo, Jeff T. Larsen, and Tanya L. Chartrand. 2003. "May I Have Your Attention, Please: Electrocortical Responses to Positive and Negative Stimuli." *Neuropsychologia* 41 (2): 171–83.

Smith, Philip. 2005. *Why War? The Cultural Logic of Iraq, the Gulf War, and Suez.* Chicago: University of Chicago Press.

———. 2008. *Punishment and Culture.* Chicago: University of Chicago Press.

Snow, David, Burke Rochford, Steven Worden, and Robert Benford. 1986. "Frame Alignment Processes, Micromobilization, and Movement Participation." *American Sociological Review* 51 (4): 464–81.

Somers, Margaret R. 1994. "The Narrative Constitution of Identity: A Relational and Network Approach." *Theory and Society* 23:605–49.

Spivak, Gayatari Chakravorty. 2013. *An Aesthetic Education in the Era of Globalization.* Cambridge, MA: Harvard University Press.

Stanley, Jason. 2015. *How Propaganda Works.* Princeton, NJ: Princeton University Press.

Stein, Jonathan, and Tim Dickinson. 2006. "Lie by Lie: A Timeline of How We Got into Iraq." *Mother Jones,* September/October. http://www.motherjones.com/politics/2011/12/leadup-iraq-war-timeline.

Steinberg, Marc. W. 1998. "Tilting the Frame: Considerations on Collective Action Framing from a Discursive Turn." *Theory and Society* 27:845–72.

Sternberg, Meir. 2001. "How Narrativity Makes a Difference." *Narrative* 9 (2): 115–22.

Stibbe, Arran. 2001. "Language, Power and the Social Construction of Animals." *Society and Animals* 9:145–61.

Strange, Jeffrey J. 2002. "How Fictional Tales Wag Real-World Beliefs: Models and Mechanisms of Narrative Influence." In *Narrative*

Impact: Social and Cognitive Foundations, edited by Melanie C. Green, Jeffrey J. Strange, and Timothy C. Brock, 263–86. Mahwah, NJ: Lawrence Erlbaum.

Strange, Jeffrey J., and Cynthia C. Leung. 1999. "How Anecdotal Accounts in News and in Fiction Can Influence Judgments of a Social Problem's Urgency, Causes, and Cures." *Personality and Social Psychology Bulletin* 25 (4): 436–49.

Strawson, Galen. 2004. "Against Narrativity." *Ratio* 17:428–52.

Sutherland, Edwin H., and Donald R. Cressey. 1974. *Criminology*. 9th ed. Philadelphia: J. B. Lippincott.

Sykes, Gresham M., and David Matza. 1957. "Techniques of Neutralization: A Theory of Delinquency." *American Sociological Review* 22:664–73.

Tan, Ed S. 1996. *Emotion and the Structure of Narrative Film: Film as an Emotion Machine*. Translated by Barbara Fasting. Mahwah, NJ: Lawrence Erlbaum.

Tannen, Deborah. 1989. *Talking Voices: Repetition, Dialogue, and Imagery in Conversational Discourse*. Cambridge: Cambridge University Press.

Taylor, Charles. 1989. *Sources of the Self: The Making of the Modern Identity*. Cambridge, MA: Harvard University Press.

Tilly, Charles. 2006. *Why?* Princeton, NJ: Princeton University Press.

Tobias, Scott. 2015. "Get in the Ring: The 10 Best Boxing-Movie Fights." *Rolling Stone*, July 2. http://www.rollingstone.com/movies/lists/get-in-the-ring-rating-10-best-boxing-movie-fights-20150722/rocky-balboa-vs-apollo-creed-rocky-1976-20150721.

Todorov, Tzvetan. 1977. *The Poetics of Prose*. Translated by Richard Howard. Oxford: Blackwell.

Tolle, Eckhart. 2006. *A New Earth: Awakening to Your Life's Purpose*. New York: Plume.

Torossian, Aram. 1937. *A Guide to Aesthetics*. Stanford, CA: Stanford University Press.

Travis, Jeremy, Bruce Western, and Steve Redburn, eds. 2014. *The Growth of Incarceration in the United States: Exploring Causes and Consequences*. Washington, DC: National Academies Press.

Ugelvik, Thomas. 2015. "The Rapist and the Proper Criminal: The Exclusion of Immoral Others as Narrative Work on the Self." In

Narrative Criminology: Understanding Stories of Crime, edited by Presser, Lois, and Sveinung Sandberg, 23–41. New York and London: New York University Press.

van Dijk, Teun A. 1992. "Discourse and the Denial of Racism." *Discourse and Society* 3 (1): 87–118.

———. 1993. *Elite Discourse and Racism.* Newbury Park, CA: Sage.

Van Marle, Fenna, and Shadd Maruna. 2010. "'Ontological Insecurity' and 'Terror Management': Linking Two Free-Floating Anxieties." *Punishment & Society* 12 (1): 7–26.

Van Stokkom, Bas. 2002. "Moral Emotions in Restorative Justice Conferences: Managing Shame, Designing Empathy." *Theoretical Criminology* 6 (3): 339–60.

West, Candace, and Don H. Zimmerman. 1987. "Doing Gender." *Gender and Society* 1 (2): 125–51.

West, Lindy. 2017. "Yes, This Is a Witch Hunt. I'm a Witch and I'm Hunting You." *New York Times*, October 17. https://www.nytimes.com/2017/10/17/opinion/columnists/weinstein-harassment-witchunt.html.

White, Hayden V. 1975. "Historicism, History, and the Figurative Imagination." *History and Theory* 14 (4): 48–67.

———. 1980. "The Value of Narrativity in the Representation of Reality." *Critical Inquiry* 7 (1): 5–27.

———. 1987. *The Content of the Form: Narrative Discourse and Historical Representation.* Baltimore: Johns Hopkins University Press.

White, Rob, and Diane Heckenberg. 2014. *Green Criminology: An Introduction to the Study of Environmental Harm.* Abingdon, UK: Routledge.

Whitehead, Colson. 2016. *The Underground Railroad.* New York: Doubleday.

Williams, Timothy, and Rhiannon Neilsen. 2016. "'They Will Rot the Society, Rot the Party, and Rot the Army': Toxification as an Ideology and Motivation for Perpetrating Violence in the Khmer Rouge Genocide?" *Terrorism and Political Violence*, October, 1–22. http://dx.doi.org.proxy.lib.utk.edu:90/10.1080/09546553.2016.1233873.

Wilson, George M. 2003. "Narrative." In *The Oxford Handbook of Aesthetics*, edited by Jerrold Levinson, 392–407. Oxford: Oxford University Press.

Wilson, James Q., and Richard J. Herrnstein. 1985. *Crime and Human Nature.* New York: Simon and Schuster.

Wilson, James Q., and George L. Kelling. 1982. "Broken Windows: The Police and Neighborhood Safety." *Atlantic Monthly* 249 (3): 29–38. https://www.theatlantic.com/magazine/archive/1982/03/broken-windows/304465/.

Wolfgang, Marvin E., and Franco Ferracuti. 1967. *The Subculture of Violence: Towards an Integrated Theory in Criminology.* London: Tavistock.

Worth, Sarah E. 2017. *In Defense of Reading.* London: Rowman and Littlefield International.

Wright, John Paul, and Kevin M. Beaver. 2005. "Do Parents Matter in Creating Self-Control in Their Children? A Genetically Informed Test of Gottfredson and Hirschi's Theory of Low Self-Control." *Criminology* 43 (4): 1169–202.

Yochelson, Samuel, and Stanton E. Samenow. 1976. *The Criminal Personality: A Profile for Change.* New York: Jason Aronson.

Young, Jock. 2003. "Merton with Energy, Katz with Structure: The Sociology of Vindictiveness and the Criminology of Transgression." *Theoretical Criminology* 7 (3): 389–414.

———. 2011. *The Criminological Imagination.* Cambridge, UK: Polity Press.

Zerubavel, Eviatar. 1997. *Social Mindscapes: An Invitation to Cognitive Sociology.* Cambridge, MA: Harvard University Press.

Zimbardo, Philip G. 1970. "The Human Choice: Individuation, Reason, and Order versus Deindividuation, Impulse, and Chaos." In *Nebraska Symposium on Motivation, 1969*, edited by William J. Arnold and David Levine, 237–307. Lincoln: University of Nebraska Press..

INDEX

Made in the USA
Middletown, DE
04 April 2021